SEATON AND EAST DEVON
IN THE SECOND WORLD WAR

*Dedicated to Lyn & Geoff Marshall
who did all the hard work*

SEATON AND EAST DEVON IN THE SECOND WORLD WAR

TED GOSLING

FONTHILL

Fonthill Media Limited
www.fonthillmedia.com
office@fonthillmedia.com

First published in the United Kingdom 2014

British Library Cataloguing in Publication Data:
A catalogue record for this book is available from the British Library

Copyright © Ted Gosling 2014

ISBN 978 1 78155 429 6

The right of Ted Gosling to be identified as the author of this work has been asserted by him in accordance with the Copyright, Designs and Patents Act 1988.

All rights reserved. No part of this publication may be reproduced, stored in a retrieval system or transmitted in any form or by any means, electronic, mechanical, photocopying, recording or otherwise, without prior permission in writing from Fonthill Media Limited

Typeset in Sabon LT
Printed and bound by CPI Group (UK) Ltd, Croydon, CR0 4YY

Contents

	Introduction	7
1	Our Finest Hour	9
2	From Foreign Shore	34
3	Some Personal Recollections of American Soldiers in Seaton and Other Memories of Seaton during the Second World War	51
4	Those Who Served	79
5	Nestlecombe and BranscombeThe War Years	101
6	Sidmouth	107
7	Small Talk from Seaton — Ted Gosling and Gerald Gosling Remember	112
8	The Final Victory	120
	Conclusion	123
	Acknowledgements	127

Introduction

When I was asked to write a Foreword for this book I reflected on how fortunate we are to have a historian in our midst who continues to document and preserve for us our rich history. Ted Gosling has done it again with this book, capturing and recording recollections of local people and the history of Seaton and the surrounding areas during World War Two, from 1939–1945. Ted's own recollections as a young lad growing up in Seaton are a window into a different era. Community spirit is alive and well in Seaton but what a demonstration of community spirit it was when a trench the length of the beach was dug by local people, young and old, to prevent the enemy from landing on our beach.

Seaton should be proud of its past and the men and women who lived and worked in Seaton and East Devon during that time. Many left, fought in the war and paid the ultimate price. Their sacrifices enable us to live the lives we live today in freedom and peace. Many local names are recorded on the memorial at St Gregory's Church so that we remember the fallen. We are indebted to the Seaton Branch of the Royal British Legion who lead us on Remembrance Day each year in remembering the fallen from all wars.

We thank those who joined us fleetingly in Seaton, for various reasons during the war, particularly the American Army who were stationed in Seaton.

This book is full of real stories of how it was for local families, the loss, hardship, the joys and the sheer bravery and determination of many local men and women.

Seaton thanks you, Ted Gosling for bringing the past to life so that we never forget.

Cllr Gaynor Sedgwick
Seaton Town Mayor
March 2014

1
Our Finest Hour

Although not in the front line of the Second World War, Seaton had its share of privation. It was home to many evacuees, some of whom stayed in the area after the war. The town was also the site of an internment camp, and home to soldiers from many lands, some of whom were killed fighting for the British cause. Seaton families also lost sons to the war, many of them in heroic circumstances. It was a time when the community came together in a way which had not been seen before or since.

The era that commenced with the Depression of 1930 ended in 1939 with war. Following a short period of relief from the mounting tension felt across the whole country, when Prime Minister Chamberlain returned home in 1938 from his meeting with Hitler in Munich declaring 'peace in our time', there came a realisation in 1939 that war was inevitable. Just before the outbreak of hostilities, young men from Seaton, Beer and Branscombe were attending the summer camp of the 4th Battalion Devonshire Regiment (Territorials) at Corfe. They were volunteers, and these summer training camps were a chance to enjoy a break from everyday life together with local friends. They were to return home to witness all the illusions and hopes of the 1930s finally disappear when, with the people of Seaton, they heard Mr Chamberlain speaking over the radio, saying in a strained voice that we were at war with Germany.

One of the first incidents of the Second World War that had a direct impact on the town of Seaton occurred on Sunday 17 September 1939 when the aircraft-carrier HMS *Courageous* was sunk by a German U-boat (*U29*) in the Atlantic, to the west of Ireland. A total of 519 of her crew perished, including her Captain, W. T. Makeig Jones, a Seaton man. John Wells, also from Seaton, had joined the Navy as a boy seaman in 1938, and he was serving on the *Courageous*. But Wells managed to escape by climbing through a porthole. Shortly after this dramatic episode in his

Seaton and East Devon in the Second World War

Between the wars the camping out of the Territorials at important points of the countryside enlivened rural England and added to the pleasures of a soldier's life. In the summer of 1937, just before the outbreak of the Second World War, the 4th Battalion Devonshire Regt Territorials held their camp at Corfe, and here we see them on the march. Young men from Seaton, Branscombe and Sidmouth attended this camp and for them it was a chance to get a break from everyday life together with local friends.

life, John Wells paid a visit to his old Seaton school Sir Walter Trevelyan's, where, after he had been introduced by the headmaster, John Webby, he related his experience to the enthralled pupils.

SEATON'S INTERNMENT CAMP

An early physical manifestation of the arrival of the war in Seaton occurred when Warner's Holiday Camp was requisitioned by the government and re-opened in October 1939 as an internment camp for classified aliens.

A high, barbed-wire fence was erected around the camp, and the guards included local Territorials. Many of the internees were to die during the spring of 1940 when they were deported to Canada on board the ship that had, in the pre-war period, been a luxury liner: the *Andorra Star*. This liner was torpedoed and sunk by a German U-boat in the Atlantic.

One of the internees who escaped this fate, however, was the famous anti-Nazi lawyer and journalist, Sebastian Haffner. He remained in the Warner's Holiday Camp until April 1940, when he was released following representations to the Home Office. Haffner remained in London, working for the *Observer* newspaper until 1954. He then went back to Germany and wrote for *Die Welt* and for *Stern* magazine. He was the author of

A few days after the outbreak of the Second World War, the campers at Warner's Holiday Camp had packed up and left the site, ready for it to be used as an internment camp. Barbed wire fencing was erected around the camp, and these Army lads from Branscombe were on guard duty after the internees had arrived. Left to right: George Gratton, Norman Somers, Nobby Clarke and Ger Abbot.

several historical bestsellers, including *The Rise and Fall of Prussia, From Bismarck to Hitler* and *The Meaning of Hitler,* which sold nearly one million copies. In fact, Haffner died only recently, in 1999, aged ninety-one. A manuscript found by his son after his death was recently published as a book entitled *Defying Hitler.* It is said that no other book has ever explained so clearly how it was possible for the Nazis to gain a foothold and make a whole nation into a pack of hunting hounds, directed against humans.

THE ARRIVAL OF EVACUEES

Shortly after the outbreak of war in September 1939, long lines of children could be seen in the cities of Britain, making their way to the railway stations for evacuation to the country. Over a four-day period, 4,000 trains were used to transport more than 1,300,000 evacuees. This was a remarkable undertaking and much credit was due to the organisers. The evacuees who arrived in Seaton were almost certainly met by Mr Brewer, the Billeting Officer, who had the difficult task of quickly placing the children in suitable homes; many of these new arrivals were to remain in Seaton for the rest of their lives.

In October 1940, 150 more evacuees from the East End of London arrived at only twelve hours' notice. Once again Mr Brewer assisted by members of voluntary organisations, achieved wonders. One of the evacuees was a young Terry Scales, who came from South London. His first shock was trying to understand the speech of the locals, who seemed to converse in a strange language, using words such as 'dasn't', 'casn't', 'thake'—closer to the English of the time of James I than the language of London in the twentieth century with which he was familiar. However, Terry Scales' years in Seaton proved a long adventure, and probably the most significant experience in his life. Being so closely in touch with nature in rural Devon seemed to sow the seeds of his future career—that of a landscape painter. Other evacuees included the Baker family, the Pritchards, Soapy Hudson and his sister, Jim Thomas, Alfie Gillett and his sister, and many others.

Our Finest Hour

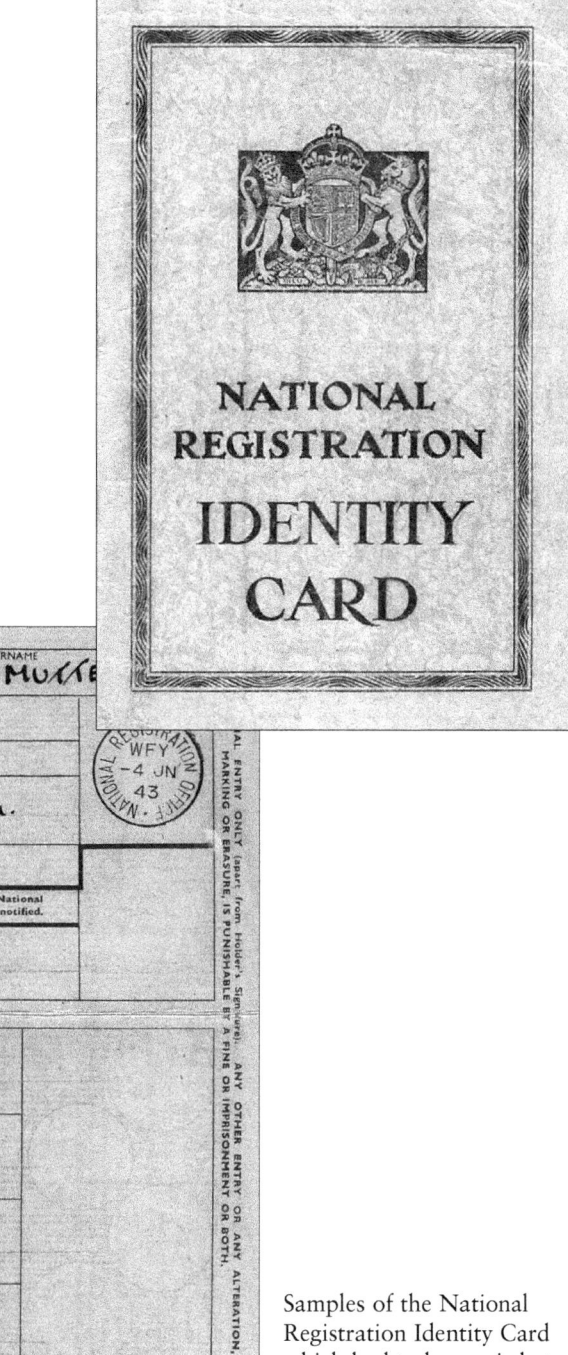

Samples of the National Registration Identity Card which had to be carried at all times.

13

Mr E. D. Brewer, Billeting Officer, with Mrs. Brewer and Nina in the back garden of 7 Havenview Road, 1944-45.

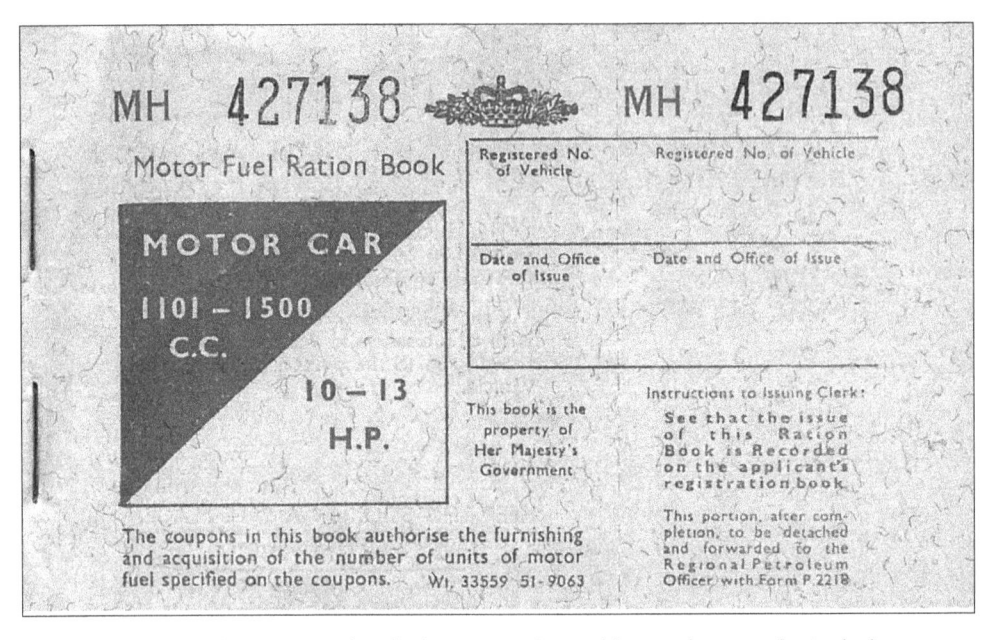

A Motor Fuel Ration Book, which contained monthly vouchers to obtain fuel.

By the end of 1940, the flood of evacuees to Seaton was so great that the main school, Sir Walter Trevelyan, could no longer cope and other centres, like the Congregational Church Hall in Cross Street and the church rooms on the Colyford Road, were commandeered. John Webby was then the much-loved headmaster of Trevelyan School. He was a teacher of outstanding ability and an absolute disciplinarian. When boys were ordered to the front of his class for punishment, they knew they deserved all they would get.

Mary W. Smith née McKeon has memories of the Children's Overseas Reception Board:

> In June 1940 the Government set up CORB (Children's Overseas Reception Board) to plan and carry out the evacuation of children between the ages of five and fifteen to the Dominions. My brother and I were two of the children chosen to go to Canada—we were five and ten years respectively.
>
> We set off from Bournemouth and travelled to Liverpool. After a short stay in Liverpool we boarded the SS *Volendam*, a Dutch ship of the Holland/America line, on 29 August. There were 606 passengers on board including 320 children.
>
> The ship left Liverpool, in convoy, under darkness, in the early morning, but the same night at 2200 hours, torpedoes were fired at the ship by a German U-boat and an emergency drill took place. The lifeboats were launched into the sea, which was very rough. Eventually everyone was rescued by other ships in the convoy and we were picked up by an oil tanker.
>
> We travelled back to Greenock on the Clyde, where we were given food and clothing, and then transported by train back home to Bournemouth, expecting to try again to go to Canada. Unfortunately a short time later a second ship—the *City of Benares*—was torpedoed with massive loss of life, and the CORB scheme was cancelled.

Most local industries of East Devon continued throughout the Second World War, but the emphasis was on war production. Early in the war an ammunition factory was established at Branscombe, when the owner of a London factory who had secured a government contract moved his factory's machinery to the Nestlé factory in Branscombe Square. The production of shell fuses and aircraft components increased and at one time 114 people were employed working 12-hour shifts. The shell fuses were loaded into a van and delivered to Seaton railway station.

At Beer, the stone quarries were used by the Admiralty as an ammunition store, with the ceilings of the many tunnels being lined with asbestos sheeting. In the centre of Beer village, the large motor garage belonging to C. R. Good & Son was requisitioned, and taken over by the Gundry Company at Bridport. It was used as a factory for making all types of nets for the Admiralty. Outwork was organised in the fishermen's cottages around the village, and both men and women produced hand-made nets. Shands came down from London and took over half of the Axminster Carpet factory, manufacturing machine tools and printing type, while carpets were still woven in the other half.

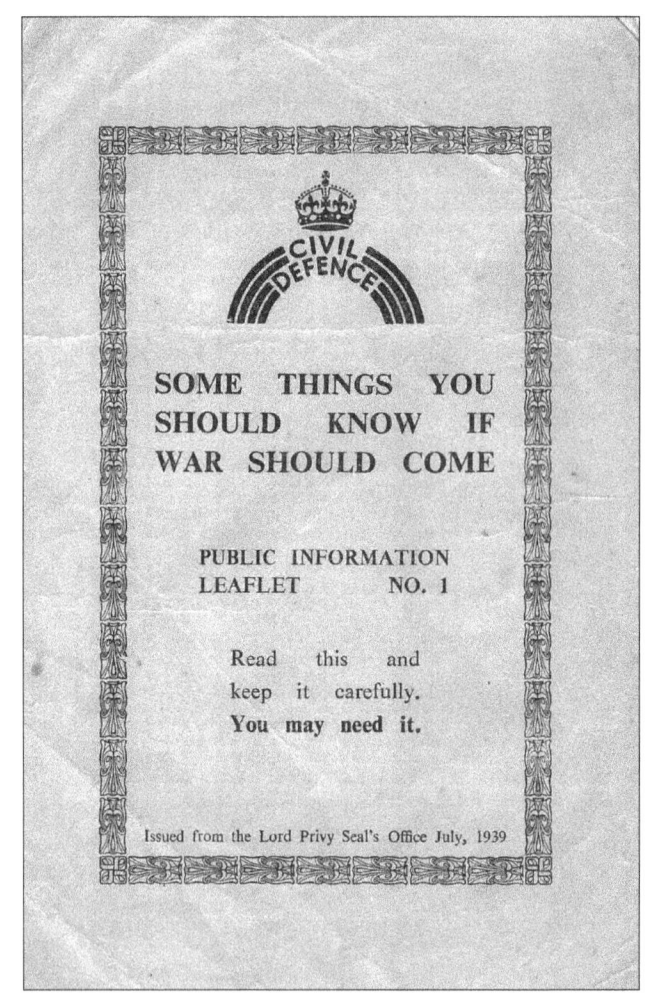

Public Information Leaflet No. 1, 1939, gives information on what to do in case of an air raid warning, and how to look after your gas mask. It also gives advice on lighting restrictions and fire precautions.

Frank Elston, right, with war production team at Hellier's garage, Honiton, during the 1939-45 war.

Farmers were encouraged to produce more food and were helped by the land girls of the Women's Land Army, who ploughed and harvested to help keep the nation from starvation. Children from the local schools were employed to dig up potatoes in the fields, while the fishermen along the coast continued to carry on their hazardous occupation.

SEATON DIRECTLY EXPERIENCE THE WAR

The first months of the Second World War became known as 'the phoney war'. However, this period ended abruptly in April 1940 with the German invasion of Holland and Denmark, and France fell. Disaster followed disaster and, after evacuating her forces at Dunkirk, Britain stood alone. It was then that the people of Seaton became unified as never before, or indeed since. Churchill had made that famous and magnificent speech, 'We shall fight them on the beaches . . .' and, in response, on a hot weekend in

June, everyone in the town, from the very young to the very old, assembled on Seaton beach to dig a trench as a first defence against the threatened invasion. This, indeed, was their finest hour.

In 1840, in early Victorian times, Seaton had been a community of just 765 people who were, in many ways, 'cut off' from the outside world. Since that date, waves of change had broken over this Devon town. Thus, while its contribution to national events had been minimal, occasionally distant rumbles from the outside world had been heard.

However, it was not really until 1940 that the people of Seaton faced a major threat – they were ready – they had come of age. By the beginning of June, most of Western Europe had fallen to the might of the well-equipped and well-trained German army. Many people thought that we had lost the war when suddenly, with force and language, Winston Churchill, employing his ornate phraseology and his instinctive feel for Britain's glorious past, made millions dare to hope again. People in Seaton who were alive at that time will well remember Churchill's speeches broadcast on the radio, which made listeners feel a part of that glorious time in history. His voice sent shivers down the spine and few could forget the experience of hearing him.

During the period from August 1940 until 1943, East Devon was subjected to many air raids. Seaton was the target for hit-and-run German raiders who were attempting to destroy the naval gun on Cliff Field, which was disguised as a small house. Unfortunately, another house nearby, at the corner of Seahill and Castle Hill, was hit and demolished, resulting in the death of Major Cartwright and his family, who were having lunch at the time.

Other bombs fell in Highwell Road and Harepath Road, where Mrs Walton, widow of the church organist, and two evacuee girls were killed. As a protection against these sudden air raids, a shelter was built beside the Church of the Good Shepherd for the use of the townspeople. Late one Saturday evening in 1944, after an air raid warning, a German aircraft being chased out to sea jettisoned its load of 1,000 lb bombs to facilitate its escape. Mrs Irene Fox, standing at her front bedroom window in Westmead, Seaton Down Road, thought the loud swish was a plane brushing the tall trees in Florrie Erskine's garden behind Westmead. In fact, two bombs had fallen within feet of each other on either side of the dividing fence at the bottom of the garden. The ARP Warden soon arrived and told the Fox family that they and other neighbours must evacuate the premises. Mrs Fox's son, Ray, was away on a Colyton Boy Scout Camp and did not know of the incident until Church Parade the next day, when he was greeted by the Revd H. R. Cooke with the words, 'Ah Fox, a bomb fell on your home

Unexploded bomb at Seaton.

last night but fortunately it didn't go off!' The bomb disposal team spent some days digging down and defusing the bomb.

SPY SAGA AT SEATON

Mike Tennent of Esher, Surrey recalled an incident in 1940:

> As an eleven year old, and an only child, the summer of 1940 saw me driving, with my mother at the wheel, westward from Sussex. My father, an army officer of the First World War, was again in uniform and was becoming increasingly worried that Germans might be dropped by parachute on to the South Downs behind where we lived. He ordered my mother immediately to evacuate the two of us down to the West Country.
>   My mother sought the help of her sister's husband, a doctor who had been called up into the army and was then the senior medical officer at Seaton, where the holiday camp had been turned into a prisoner-of-war camp. The camp housed, amongst others, U-boat commanders, who were considered to be amongst the most belligerent of prisoners. My uncle, having once been attacked by such a prisoner, told us he now kept a loaded revolver in his surgery desk drawer!

My uncle suggested we break our journey westwards by stopping a few days at Seaton. We agreed and he deliberately booked us into a back room of a particular hotel on the front, and came round to see us soon after we arrived. Because of my age I was not immediately let into the secret discussion he had with my mother.

My uncle had been billeted in a small cottage at the back of Seaton, from where he and my aunt overlooked the camp. It was my uncle's custom, before going to bed, to sit outside his cottage for a last smoke. Recently, his attention had been drawn to what he took to be a flashing light coming from the back of our hotel. The light seemed to be aimed at the camp, but my uncle was not located such that he could see if there were any flashing replies. He asked my mother if she would see if she could identify the window the flashes were coming from, and then try to find out which guest occupied that bedroom.

It was late and, as soon as we had dressed for bed that evening, my mother turned off the light and pulled back the curtains. No flashes appeared. My mother decided next evening we should come up to our room immediately after dinner. This we did, and had a grandstand view of Morse code being flashed from the hotel, two windows away from our own, and replies coming back from the camp. At breakfast the next day my mother's suspicions fell on two ladies sitting at single tables in the dining room, and she later got into conversation with one of them in the lounge.

My mother had judged well, and found the lady very willing to talk. She told my mother how she had bought herself a cottage up on the east side of Seaton, which was now being decorated ready for her to move into. Before leaving our Sussex home my mother had read in the paper that it was customary for German spies to paint their 'safe houses' a certain shade of pink. Armed with this information, my mother questioned the lady about her choice of colour. Pink she replied, and even brought a colour specimen out of her handbag. She went on to tell my mother she was having the well in the garden cleared and some alterations carried out indoors.

All of this was faithfully relayed back to my uncle, who took it up with the appropriate authorities. Meanwhile, it was time for my mother and myself to head further westwards. In Seaton, a close watch was kept on the camp, the cottage and the lady, especially when, one evening, German planes were heard flying low over the neighbourhood. Suspicions of an imminent break-out from the camp led to the cottage being raided. The well in the garden and the various newly-built partitions indoors were found to be stacked with machine guns and ammunition, no doubt dropped by the German planes on the hills behind Seaton and carried by local spies to the lady's cottage. The lady herself was interned for the remainder of the war.

The voluntary services were quickly organised for the national emergency. An appeal broadcast in May 1940 for volunteers for the Local Defence Volunteers had hardly ended before hundreds of East Devonians were queuing at Post Offices to be registered. Later the LDV was reorganised and renamed the Home Guard. The men soon went into rigorous training, with drills and parades, midnight exercises over the cliffs, guard and picket duties in lonely spots, all making ready to be called out for their primary purpose, defence against invasion.

The men of Seaton's Home Guard (at first known as the Local Defence Volunteers) who played such a crucial and much appreciated role in the town during the difficult war years.

YOUR FOOD IN WAR-TIME

PUBLIC INFORMATION LEAFLET   NO. 4

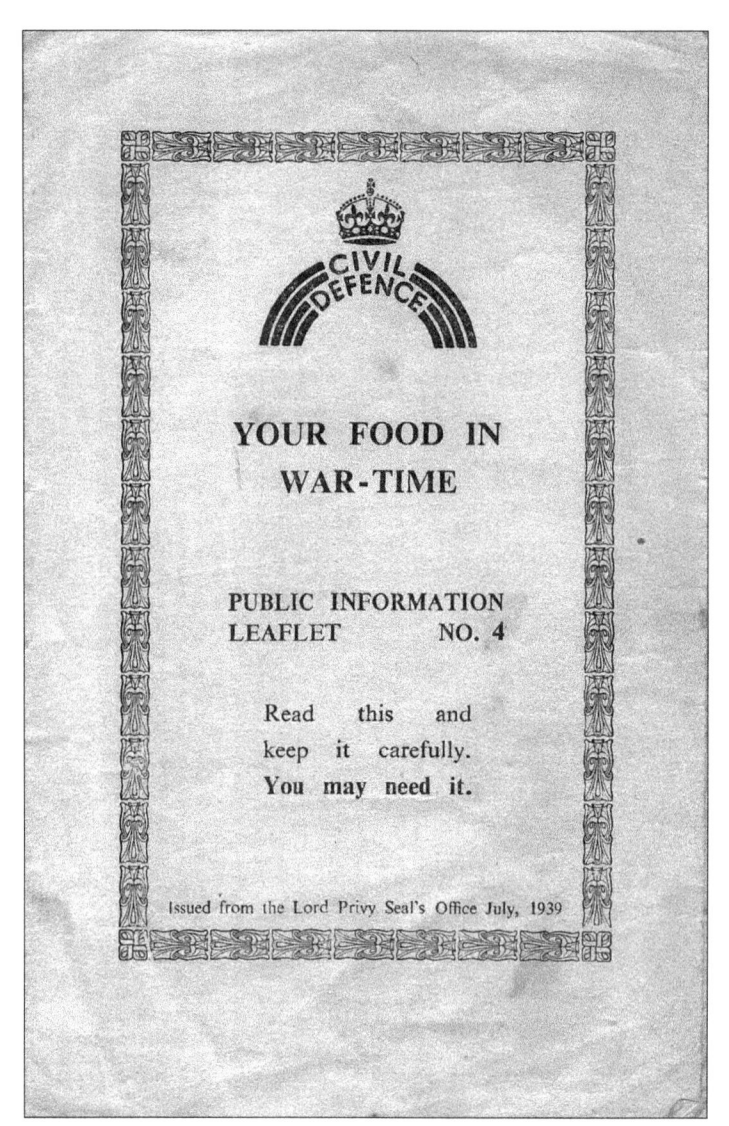

Read this and keep it carefully. **You may need it.**

Issued from the Lord Privy Seal's Office July, 1939

Many Public Information Leaflets were issued in wartime. This 1939 leaflet, Your Food in War-time, advises how to store food safely, and warns that rationing may become necessary.

The National Fire Service, Rescue Squads, Police and Special Constabulary were also turning out on every alert. The firemen in particular were not confined to local incidents, being called away to render help in Exeter and Plymouth when those cities were blitzed.

The Observer Corps was formed and lookout towers built along the coast. For five years they kept continuous watch, day and night, reporting all aircraft movements. Raiders passed over East Devon to attack places as

Axmouth Home Guard c. 1942. Back row, left to right: Jeff Puddicombe, Gordon Hunt, Ray Hunt, Leslie Hunt, Mr Mann Sr, Mr Mann Jr. Middle row: Herbie Clements, Jack Good, Ted Snell, Jim Cross, Jim Board, Ken Morgan, Mr Mann. Front row: Frank Snell, Harry Newbery, Len Weekes, Revd Mr Swift, Howie Owen, Ken Webber, Victor Worden.

remote as Liverpool and Belfast, and in these cases the alert would last all night, until the planes returned on their way back to Northern Europe. On one occasion the Exmouth observer post on Orcombe Point was machine-gunned by a Dornier and showered with a stick of incendiary bombs, but without injury to those on duty.

The Air Raid Precautions Committee was also busy. In Exmouth it appealed for 600 volunteers and soon afterwards had distributed 27,000 gas masks, and 22 air raid shelters were erected with accommodation for over 1,000 people. The Library in Exeter Road was requisitioned for the ARP Headquarters and Control Centre, and altogether some 1,300 alerts

Seaton AFC Fire, 1939–45.

and incidents were dealt with by the mixed staff on duty. They ranged from elderly men to women telephonists and young messenger boys.

Many other organisations, including the Women's Voluntary Service, YMCA, Salvation Army and the Voluntary Aid Detachment nurses, played their part magnificently throughout the war.

At the outbreak of war, there were more than 1,400 local fire authorities in England and Wales and these were consolidated into single national fire service, giving the advantage of greater mobility and a universal standard of training and equipment. The skilful dedication of Seaton's National Fire Service during the war must never be forgotten – they played a heroic part in the defence of Exeter against enemy bombing and were at hand when hit-and-run raiders dropped bombs on Seaton.

During the Second World War, Devon became one of the most militarily active counties in the United Kingdom. The county suffered from bombs, landmines and shells. Despite all this, the inhabitants endeavoured to carry on their everyday life as normally as possible.

Wartime bus conductresses, Dorothy Andrews and Peg Seager, with driver, Giles White (of Beer) at Seaton's Station Road bus depot in 1942. Seaton's women played a vital role in civil defence and keeping the town's services running during the Second World War.

The first major event to affect them was the evacuation of Dunkirk in May 1940. The unexpected stationing of troops, including the Kings Own Infantry regiment, in East Devon brought home to local residents the fact that things were becoming very serious, and an invasion by the Germans was imminent. The people became used to seeing a strong Army presence in the area, while the RAF set up permanent camps and built the advance radar station on Beer Head. The aerodrome at Honiton Clyst was taken over by the RAF and new airfields were constructed at Dunkeswell and Smeatharpe. The Navy was responsible for defence work in the river estuaries while an RAF air-sea rescue unit was established at Lyme Regis, just over the border in Dorset.

During the period from August 1940 to early 1943 East Devon was subject to many air raids. In 1942, during a night attack on Exeter, a German plane was shot down over Beer, one of its engines landing in a field

Members of the National Fire Service, Seaton *c.* 1943. At the outbreak of war there were more than 1,400 local fire authorities in England and Wales. These were consolidated into a single National Fire Service, giving the advantages of greater mobility and a universal standard of training and equipment. These firemen played a heroic part in the defence of Exeter and Plymouth during enemy bombing.

on one side of the village, with the main part of the plane crashing in Bovey Lane. The crew had parachuted to safety, landing on Beer Common where they were quickly picked up by the Home Guard. On another occasion a lone Messerschmitt 109 strafed and machine-gunned Colyton; fragments of the shells are still occasionally found around the houses at Hillhead. Seaton was the target of hit-and-run German raiders who were attempting to destroy the naval gun on Cliff Field, which was disguised as a small house. An air-raid shelter was built in front of the Church of the Good Shepherd for the use of the townspeople.

A landing craft was beached at Seaton after returning from the D-Day landings. On 26 February 1943 Exmouth experienced its last air raid. Eight Focke-Wulf fighter bombers, sneaking in over the town in daylight, killed about twenty-five men and women, as well as a little girl.

In Sidmouth more than five hundred air raid alerts were sounded. The town was occasionally machine-gunned from the air and sometimes enemy pilots dropped bombs on Sidmouth that had been intended for Exeter. A coastal defence battery was established in the Connaught Gardens, and Army and RAF contingents were stationed in the town. The grounds of the Knowle Hotel were used as a training area for commandos.

Special War Savings weeks were held at intervals throughout East Devon between 1941 and 1945; these comprised War Weapons Week, Warship Week, Wings for Victory Week, Salute the Soldier Week and Thanksgiving Week. Exmouth raised over £4 million pounds altogether.

In 1940 the RAF came to the area and no. 13 Radar Station was built on Beer Head, with a prominent wooden tower and mast. Early in the war, radar was our secret weapon, and it provided early warning of the approach of enemy planes. The unit at Beer was the first to make contact

Wartime picture, 1942. The False House that hid the 2.6-inch naval guns and 100 shells on West Cliff, Seaton.

with Mr Churchill returning in his plane from his important meeting with President Roosevelt. A subsidiary camp for housing the RAF personnel was built at nearby Weston, the centre of which being where Stoneleigh Holiday Centre stands today.

Beach and coastal defences were erected along the coast. Seaton was guarded by two 6-inch naval guns of no. 402 Coastal Battery. At Sidmouth the Coastal Battery was equipped with one naval gun and one French gun, both of First World War vintage, and a 16-pounder gun. At Exmouth the swing bridge and wooden jetty were immobilised each night. Tank traps, concrete anti-tank defences and pillboxes were erected. The pillbox was a means of static defence against enemy infantry forces. Old cars were dispersed on Honiton Common to prevent enemy aircraft or gliders landing.

In May 1941 Rudolph Hess landed in Scotland, causing considerable national interest; less well known was his connection with East Devon. His father had married his first wife at Exmouth, and on her death she was buried in the local churchyard.

Coastal defence guns, several of First World War vintage were erected at prominent points along the coast. The appearance of anti-aircraft guns, searchlights and sound locators in fields or on the hills was the next development, while the Army hastily dug trenches, laid mines, and erected scaffolding and barbed wire entanglements along the pebble beaches. Concrete blockhouses were built along likely paths of advance by invading forces.

Seaton was fortunate during the war to have a vicar who knew the horrors of war first hand. Revd Harry Cooke had won the Military Cross in the First World War and was a natural leader of men. His wife, Norah, was also a war heroine in her own right, having served as a VAD nurse and survived the sinking of the hospital ship, *Britannia*, in the Gulf of Athens in November 1916. Revd Cooke led the town in many of the national days of prayer; he was, with his Christian faith, a source of comfort to many people in Seaton during those difficult times.

Throughout the war years, a most charming and gentle Portuguese-born priest, Father Ortiz, served at St Augustine's Catholic Church in Manor Road. Although he spoke very little English, he was much loved by all for his sympathy for the British in our time of danger. The Catholic community in Seaton at that time was small but, by contrast, the Gospel Hall attracted many stalwart worshippers who were led in prayer by Mr A. S. Ferris and Mr Ben Turner. In fact, the War years brought the followers of all of the town's religions closer together, showing a tolerance towards each other.

Dick Wilkins, pictured on Seaton sea front, 1941. In this rare wartime photograph the concrete anti-tank defences can be seen.

As noted already, the chairman of Seaton Urban District Council during the war was Frank Norcombe. He was probably the most able council chairman that the town has ever had and proved to be the right man for the job at a time of immense difficulty and challenge.

DIGGING FOR VICTORY AND THE CAMPAIGN ON THE HOME FRONT

By the end of 1940, strict food rationing was introduced and people were encouraged to 'dig for victory' by growing their own food in their gardens and allotments. Blackout material was in great demand to cover the windows at night, and strict control was exercised on householders by the ARP and the special constabulary. The people of Seaton were issued

Seaton and East Devon in the Second World War

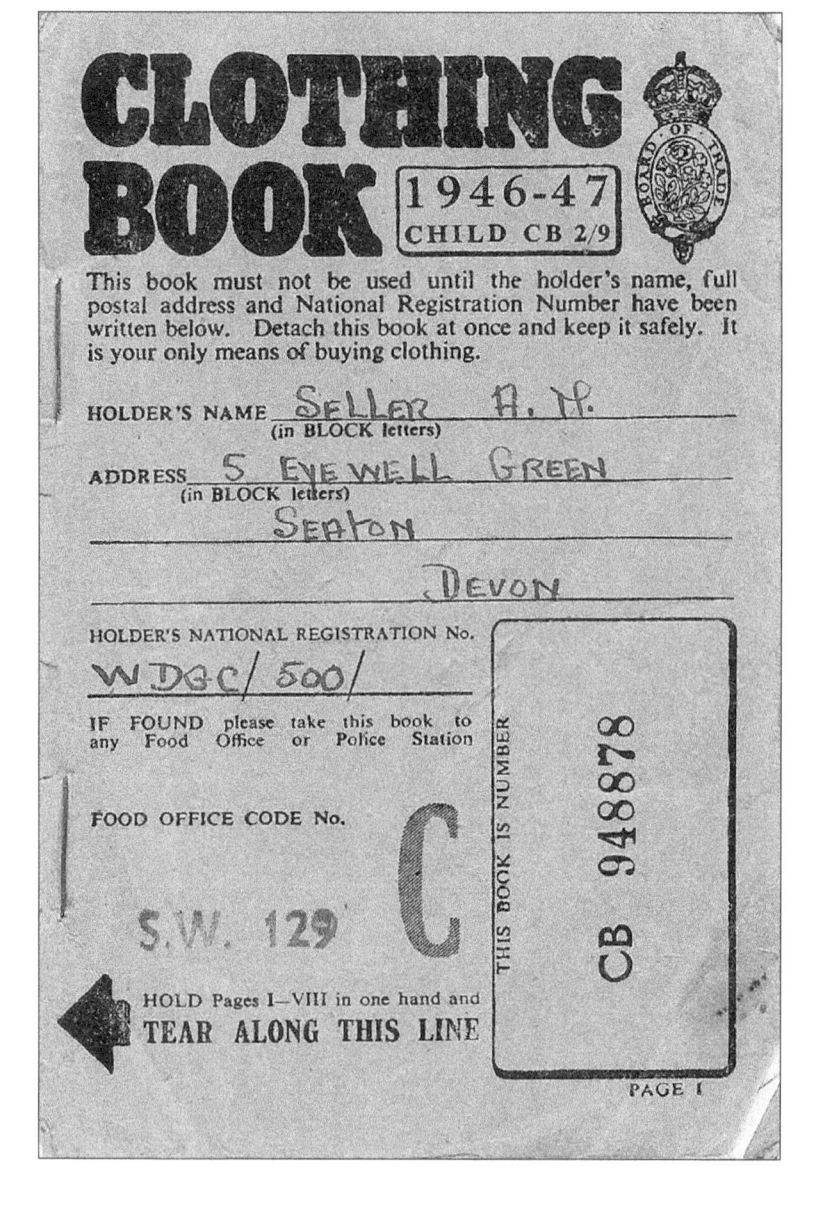

RATIONING OF CLOTHING: NUMBER OF COUPONS NEEDED

On June 1, Mr. Oliver Lyttelton, President of the Board of Trade (below, left), announced his scheme for the immediate rationing of clothing, including footwear. Each person will have 66 clothing coupons to last for twelve months

MEN and BOYS	Adult	Child		WOMEN and GIRLS	Adult	Child
ined mackintosh or cape	9	7		Lined mackintoshes, or coats (over 28 in. long)	14	11
er mackintoshes, or raincoat, or overcoat	16	11		Jacket, or short coat (under 28 in. long)	11	8
t, or jacket, or blazer or like garment	13	8		Dress, or gown, or frock—woollen	11	8
istcoat, or pull-over, or cardigan, or jersey	5	3		Dress, or gown, or frock—other material	7	5
users (other than fustian or corduroy)	8	6		Gym tunic, or girl's skirt with bodice	8	6
tian or corduroy trousers	5	5		Blouse, or sports shirt, or cardigan, or jumper	5	3
rts	5	3		Skirt, or divided skirt	7	5
ralls, or dungarees or like garment	6	4		Overalls, or dungarees or like garment	6	4
ssing-gown or bathing-gown	8	6		Apron, or pinafore	3	2
htshirt or pair of pyjamas	8	6		Pyjamas	8	6
t, or combinations—woollen	8	6		Nightdress	6	5
t, or combinations—other material	5	4		Petticoat, or slip, or combination, or cami-knickers	4	3
ts, or vest, or bathing costume, or child's blouse	4	2		Other undergarments, including corsets	3	2
of socks or stockings	3	1		Pair of stockings	2	1
ar, or tie, or pair of cuffs	1	1		Pair of socks (ankle length)	1	1
handkerchiefs	1	1		Collar, or tie, or pair of cuffs	1	1
f, or pair of gloves or mittens	2	2		Two handkerchiefs	1	1
of slippers or goloshes	4	2		Scarf, or pair of gloves or mittens, or muff	2	2
of boots or shoes	7	3		Pair of slippers, boots or shoes	5	3
of leggings, gaiters or spats	3	2				

LOTH. Coupons needed per yard depend on the width. KNITTING WOOL. 1 coupon for two ounces.

CIVIL DEFENCE

EVACUATION
WHY AND HOW?

PUBLIC INFORMATION
LEAFLET   NO. 3

Read this and keep it carefully. **You may need it.**

Issued from the Lord Privy Seal's Office July, 1939

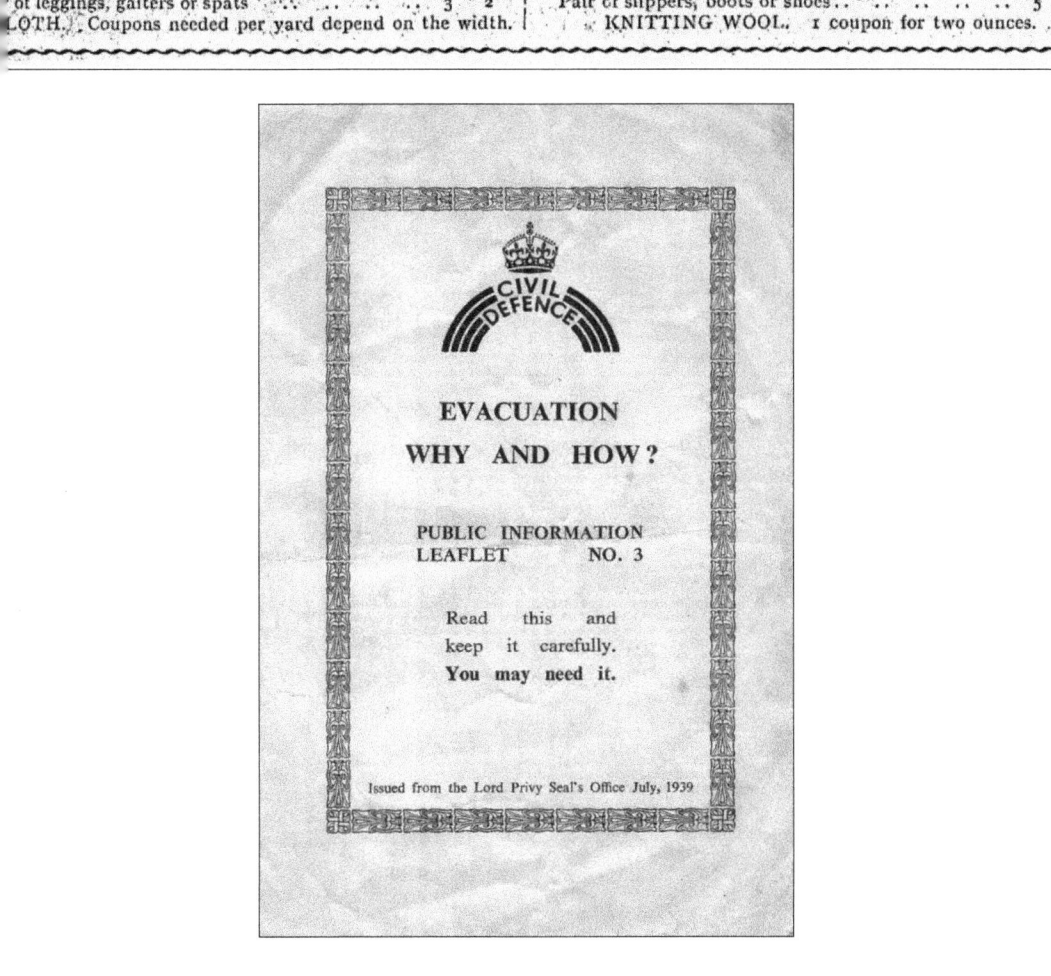

WINGS FOR VICTORY

SEATON, COLYTON, BEER and DISTR[ICT]

including

AXMOUTH, BRANSCOMBE, COM[BPYNE]
COLYFORD, ROUSDON, SOUT[H]
and WESTON.

May 22nd to 29th,

TARGET - £50,0[00]

1 BOMBER and 2 TYPH[OONS]

Official Opening on the Seafront, S[eaton]
MAY 22nd at 2 p.m. by

WING COMMANDER [

supported by C. DREWE, ESQ., M.P., [
the Council and other Guests. Pr[
Parade of the Fighting Services and [
Services led by the Band of th[e

BADGES ON SALE ALL THE [WEEK
EXHIBITION BOMB for affixing Stamp[s
Centre, Electricity Offices, Se[

SETTING OF THE INDICATOR wil[l
3 p.m. daily. Please turn up and see [
being smashed.

WINGS FOR VICTORY

COLYTON.

SATURDAY, MAY 22nd. OPENING DAY. 6 p.m. Grand Parade and March Past by all Local Organisations, led by the Seaton Scout Band. Official Opening by C. DREWE, ESQ., M.P. and other Speakers.
Dance in The Town Hall. 8 to 11.45 p.m. Admission 2/6. Forces 1/6. Whirlwind Dance Band.

MONDAY, MAY 24th. Band Concert by the Band of the Devonshire Regiment in The Town Hall. Admission 1/-. Children 6d.

TUESDAY, MAY 25th. Grand Monster Whist Drive at Town Hall at 7.30 p.m. 40 Prizes. Admission 1/6. Arranged by Women's Institute.

WEDNESDAY MAY 26th. Gigantic Old Time Social and Dance at The Town Hall. Admission 1/6. Arranged by Home Guard.

THURSDAY, MAY 27th. A.T.C. Evening at Colyton Grammar School at 7.30 p.m., concluding with Football Match, A.F.C. v. Devon Cadets. Silver Collection.

FRIDAY, MAY 28th. Concert at The Town Hall by R.A.F. Concert Party at 8 p.m. Admission 2/6, 1/6 and 1/-.

SATURDAY, MAY 29th. Childrens Grand Fancy Dress Parade and Dance. Parade at 2.15 p.m. Admission to Town Hall 6d.
Final Dance in the Town Hall. Admission 2/6. Forces 1/6. Dancing 8 to 11.45 p.m. Music by Whirlwind Dance Band.

Slogan Competition. 2 Classes. Under 18 years and over 18 years. Entries to be placed in box at Town Hall.

Mile of Pennies by 1st Colyton Troup of Scouts on 22nd.

Skittling for Pig. Competitions at White Hart, Country House and Colcombe Castle.

with identity cards, and petrol was strictly rationed through a system of coupons allocated for the few vehicles allowed on the roads. Drivers of vehicles could obtain their petrol from just a few designated garages; the only garage in the Seaton area allowed to sell petrol was Trevetts in Station Road.

Special war savings weeks were held at intervals in Seaton between 1941 and 1945. These comprised War Weapons Week, Wings for Victory Week, and Salute the Soldier Week. There are few reminders in present-day Seaton of the many thousands of troops who were stationed in the town between 1940 and 1945. Amongst them were French Canadians, units of the Free Polish and Czechoslovakian Army, the Free Spanish Army and, of course, the American troops.

Seaton's connection with the Czechoslovakian Army was acknowledged when Frank Norcombe, Chairman of the Urban District Council, and Francis Garner, Clerk to the Council, visited Dovercourt near Harwich, accompanied by their wives, in 1943. On this occasion, Frank Norcombe attached a ribbon to the colours of the 2nd Battalion of the Czech Army who were stationed at Seaton for part of the war. Some of the Czechs returned to Seaton for a visit after the war and were able to renew their acquaintance with Frank.

2

From Foreign Shore

During 1941–44 Seaton took on a Continental appearance, when Allied Czech and Polish troops were successively stationed at Warner's Holiday Camp in Harbour Road. The 2nd Battalion of the Czech Army soon won the hearts of the local people and were made most welcome.

Open-air concerts were given by the Czechoslovakian army, in front of the Esplanade Hotel, now the Hook and Parrot. We still hold in Seaton Museum a copy of the *Daily News* for the Czech troops, most of which is in Czechoslovakian except from the welcome letter from Frank Norcombe, chairman of the Seaton Urban District Council, and the thank you letter printed below. Seaton Museum would appreciate help in translating this newsletter.

During their stay in Seaton, the President of Czechoslovakia, Dr Edvard Beneš, paid them a visit. In 1943, after the Czechs had left Seaton, Frank Norcombe and Francis Garner, Clerk to Seaton Council, accompanied by their wives, visited Dovercourt, near Harwich to attach a ribbon from Seaton to the colours of the 2nd Battalion of the Czech army.

On Saturday 14 October 1972 Seaton Urban District Council and the Association of Czechoslovak Legionnaires unveiled a plaque in Seafield Gardens to commemorate the stay of Czechoslovak forces in Seaton during the Second World War.

Soon after the Czechs left, the Americans arrived.

Letter from Frank Norcombe:

I am proud and happy to be allowed to submit a few lines to your newspaper regarding the Concert given by the Czechoslovak Army Choir and Band. Words cannot express the appreciation that could be felt in the Hall, and it is an understatement to say that it was a tremendous success. I find it very difficult to mention any particular item of a programme of

Czechoslovak Army Concert:
given

ON SATURDAY, JULY 11th - 8.30 p.m.

PROGRAMME

CZECHOSLOVAK ARMY CHOIR
- Festivity Song .... B. Smetana

INTRODUCTORY REMARKS .... Lft. F.

Czechoslovak Army Choir
- If I were a little bird .... Schneider-Trnavský
- Old Tower of Trenčín .... Slovak Folk Song
- To the Devil wi' you, lads ..... Slovak Folk Song

TENOR SOLOS - CAPTAIN J. VÁLEK
- Cloves and Roses .... Czech Folk Song
- Why hurry to marry .... Slovak Folk Song
- English song
- Flower song ; Carmen .... G. Bizet

CZECHOSLOVAK CAMP BAND

INTERVAL

Czechoslovak Army Choir
- The village bells .... A. Dvořák
- The Banquet .... A. Dvořák
- Into Battle .... J. Zajc
- My precious Johnny .... F. Vránek
- The Bartered Bride, by Smetana, Arie Kecala Baso Růžička

Czechoslovak Camp Band

oooooooo

NATIONAL ANTHEMS

oooooooo

CZECHOSLOVAK ARMY CHOIR arranged and conducted by Lt. J. OBRUČA
CAMP BAND arranged and conducted by Sgt. M. MARTIN
PIANO Accompanist : Sgt. M. MARTIN

Organised by the Information Department of the CZECHOSLOVAK ARMY in conjunction with the LOCAL RED CROSS

oooooooo

OPEN AIR CONCERT will be held in front of the ESPLANADE HOTEL
6 - 7 p.m.

oooooooo

Programme for concert given by the Czechoslovak Army choir and band, on Seaton Esplanade.

Seaton and East Devon in the Second World War

Above: The Czechoslovakian President, Edvard Beneš (with entourage) on his visit to Seaton in July 1943. The occasion was to inspect his troops who were accommodated in the holiday camp. It will be recalled that some time later he met his death when he accidentally fell from a hotel balcony, in his own country. This photograph was taken by Bob Britton who, at that time, was enjoying a short leave with his wife, at the Bay Hotel.

Left: Edvard Benes in conference.

Frank Norcombe (wartime Chairman of Seaton Urban District Council) attaching a ribbon to the colours of the 2nd Battalion of the Czech Army at Dovercourt, Harwich, in 1943 to honour the Czech soldiers who had been stationed in Seaton for part of the war.

such outstanding merit, but I would say that your treatment of English songs was a real joy to everyone. I would prefer rather to say—Thank you All for something that was more than a mere Concert, IT WAS AN INSPIRATION.

I should also like to take this opportunity of thanking Lt-Col. V. P. for the invaluable assistance of his Staff Officers and Men in the organisation and the carrying out of the many jobs in connection with the Concert. Yours sincerely (signed)
F. Norcombe, Chairman of the Seaton Urban District Council.

Letter from the Officers and Men of the Czechoslovak Forces:

We would like to tell you, dear English friends that the success of our Saturday Concert is largely due to your kind collaboration. Wherever we asked for advice, we found full understanding and help. The work done

These photographs were taken in 1943, when Frank Norcombe, Chairman Seaton UDC and Francis Garner, Clerk to the Council, accompanied by their wives, visited Dovercourt, near Harwich. On this occasion, Frank Norcombe attached a Ribbon to the Colours of the 2nd Battallion of the Czech Army, who were stationed at Seaton for part of the war. Some of the Legionnaires returned for a visit to Seaton after the war, and were able to renew their acquaintance with Frank Norcombe.

The colours of the 2nd Battalion Czech Army with the ribbon from Seaton attached. It reads: 'To the 2nd Batt. Czechoslovak Army from Seaton, Devon, greetings, remembrances and gratitude.'

From Foreign Shore

The Czech Army 2nd Battalion on parade at Dover Court in 1943 during presentation of a Ribbon to their Colours by Frank Norcombe, Chairman of Seaton Urban District Council.

Frank Norcombe, with other dignitaries at Dover Court in 1943 for the presentation of a Ribbon to the Colours of the 2nd Battalion Czech Army.

by Mr. H. F. Norcombe, Chairman of the Urban District Council, by the members of the local Red Cross, by the commander of the Warner's Camp, by the NAAFI staff and practically everybody in the town, as well as the splendid generosity of our guests, has enabled the local Red Cross and ourselves to raise such a considerable sum in aid of a deserving cause.
Officers and Men of the Czechoslovak Forces.

THE AMERICANS

Following Japan's bombing and destruction of the American fleet at Pearl Harbor in December 1941, Britain gained the support of a great ally, which not only made the defeat of Nazi Germany possible, but brought thousands

From Foreign Shore

ISG Robert G. Rudman is on the right of the photograph, with two friends, in 1944. The house in the background is Haven Cliff.

American nurses who were based at the American hospital at Millwey Rise, Axminster, *c.* 1944.

of US soldiers to this country in preparation for the invasion of Europe. Winston Churchill wrote, 'no American will think it wrong of me if I proclaim that to have the United States at our side was to me the greatest joy. I knew the United States was in the war, up to the neck, and in to the death. With their help we would win the war and England would live'.

Churchill, of course, had American blood flowing in his veins, and at the time thought of a remark which Edward Grey had made to him more than thirty years before—that the United States is like a gigantic boiler. Once the fire is lighted under it, there is no limit to the power it can generate.

Many were those who came from foreign lands to build up the Allied Forces for D-Day. The Americans made the greatest impact—Dunkeswell, four miles from Honiton, was the base of the only US Naval Air Station in the United Kingdom. From this elevated East Devon airfield, the US Navy flew Liberators on anti-submarine patrols. The continuous vibration caused by the huge aircraft resulted in the tower of Dunkeswell church becoming unsafe, and having to be rebuilt. In that church is a memorial plaque to Joseph Kennedy, elder brother of the late President, John Kennedy, who lost his life on one of those patrols.

American soldiers at Colyford, 1943.

Opposite above: Members of Patrol No. 17 are waiting outside Dunkeswell Post Office to 'phone their girlfriends, in about 1944. Left to right: S/IC W. Raven in 'phone box, ARM/2C E. J. Riffin, AMM/1C E. R. Burfield, AMM/1C E. F. Stoner, AOM/2C D.H. Noodin. With a touch of glamour about their accent, and dressed in off-duty casual clothes, they must have seemed unbelievably exotic to the local girls.

Opposite below left: American soldiers pictured at Honiton Heathfield Camp, *c.* 1943.

Opposite below right: US serviceman on bike, Colyford, 1943.

From Foreign Shore

Dunkeswell was home to the US Navy Air Arm wing during the Second World War. This 1944 aerial view of the Dunkeswell dispersal area shows five parked Liberators and a Flying Fortress.

Four miles to the east of Dunkeswell, near the Somerset border, US Air Force Station 462 was opened at Smeatharpe, close to the small village of that name. The Americans took over the airfield from the RAF and used it as a base for glider training and troop carrying. On the eve of D-Day the men of the 101st Airborne Division flew from there to Normandy in eighty-one 'sky trains'.

RAF Exeter, at Clyst Honiton, became USAAF Station 463 in April 1944, and was also used for glider training. There was a large American presence in East Devon before D-Day, and the 8th Infantry Division troops

American air crew briefing in front of a bomber at wartime Dunkeswell.

were stationed at Seaton. More Americans were stationed at Heathfield Camp at Honiton. As a result of the many Americans stationed in the area, there were numerous GI brides.

An American Military Field Hospital was established at Millway Rise, Axminster, and another convalescent hospital was built alongside the water tower above Seaton.

There was a large American presence in East Devon during the months before D-Day, and the 2nd Bn, 8th Infantry were stationed at Seaton. More Americans were stationed at Honiton and indeed, on Monday 7 February 1944, General Eisenhower made a visit to the 8th Infantry at Honiton and told them he would see them all 'east of the Rhine' and would personally made certain they had champagne, 'even if I have to buy it myself'. Although we can find no evidence, it is a very strong possibility that Ike also visited Seaton.

Joseph P. Kennedy (centre rear) with his crew, Dunkeswell, summer 1944. The eldest brother of the late president, John F. Kennedy, Joseph was born in Hull, Massachusetts, on 25 July 1915. He served as a pilot in the US Navy Air Arm, flying PB4Ys (known as Liberators). On 12 August 1944, twenty-four minutes after his plane had taken off from Dunkeswell, it exploded in the air over Blythburgh, Suffolk, killing the entire crew, and with the loss to the United States of a potential president.

American soldiers were stationed at Warner's Holiday Camp, now Tesco's, and in Nissen huts on wasteland opposite the camp. Various houses were used as billets, including Seafield Terrace and Myrtle House. There was another camp of Nissen huts on the left-hand side of Beer Road, just after the junction with Old Beer Road. No. 2 Burrow Road was occupied by the American Red Cross and Ware's Garage in Harbour Road was used for motor maintenance.

To Seaton people, who had suffered years of shortage, the Americans seemed to have come from a different world, with plenty of money, plenty of food and plenty of extraordinary words. Despite this Seaton families opened their homes for American soldiers, many of whom spent time washing the dishes, helping in the garden and even becoming a handyman around the house, resulting in a greater degree of friendliness and companionship than might have happened.

The Pastimes Amusement Arcade, which kept open during the War, was very popular with the GIs and, for a reason I still cannot understand, they flocked to the local fish and chip shops. A dance was held every night in the Town Hall, and girls from miles around flocked to them. Jeeps on our streets were a familiar sight, and a centre was provided for troops in the now United Reform Church in Cross Street.

One of the officers stationed in Seaton was Captain George Mabry, who became the second most highly decorated soldier in the American military. George L. Mabry Jr., born 14 September 1917 in Stateburg, Sumter County, South Carolina, attended elementary and high school in Sumter county. He graduated from Presbyterian College, Clinton, SC, in 1940 with a BA Degree and a Reserve Commission as 2nd Lieutenant. Then he volunteered for Active Duty and joined the 2nd Battalion, 8th Infantry Regiment, 4th Infantry Division, at Harmony Church area, Fort Benning, Georgia on 5 July 1940 until January 1946. Mabry landed H-Hour D-Day on Utah Beach, 6 June 1944 with the 2nd Bn, 8th Infantry Regiment, and then fought through France, Luxembourg, Belgium and into Germany. Advanced in rank from 2nd Lieutenant, Platoon Leader to Lieutenant Colonel, Battalion commander in the 2nd Bn, 8th Infantry Regiment from 1940 to 1946. The following decorations and awards were all awarded to him during the Second World War: Medal of Honor, Distinguished Service Cross, Silver Star, Bronze Star Medal with 'V' Deice, Arrowhead and Oak Leaf Cluster, Purple Heart, Presidential Unit Citation, Distinguished Service Order (British), Belgian Fourragere, Combat Infantry Badge and five campaign medals. After thirty-five years Active Military Service, he retired as a Major General. Married, father of one daughter and two sons, and grandfather of five grandchildren, Major General George L. Mabry died on 13 July 1990.

For these young American soldiers in East Devon, war against the Nazis seemed like an adventure. Most of them were overseas for the first time, and few had any experience of combat. The baptism of fire which came on D-Day, 6 June 1944, proved to be, for them, a horrifying and unforgettable experience, when so many of these fine young men were killed.

Overall the American arrival was welcomed by the people of East Devon, who were very much aware of the crucial part that they would play in the Allied struggle.

Exercises to simulate the Normandy invasion, 'Operation Overlord', were carried out at Slapton, and one of these final dress rehearsals was code-named 'Tiger'. Sailing eastwards towards Lyme Bay, a convoy of eight vessels were simulating the time it would take to reach Normandy when, in the early hours of Friday 28 April 1944, they were attacked by German E-Boats from Cherbourg. These had managed to duck British motor torpedo boats on surveillance. The naval authorities appeared to have slipped up by sending too few escort destroyers on the exercise, and dallying over decoding a signal from British Intelligence about the E-Boat departure. Two of the American craft were torpedoed and sunk, with more than 700 Americans dead or missing. Was this a dreadful accident of war, or gross incompetence? Even today the mystery and intrigue linger on.

The beach at Slapton was ideal for simulating conditions of the actual landings on the 4th Division's beach in France. Engineers worked hard to copy the scheme of fortifications used on the shore on which the invasion landing would take place.

Twenty-seven trucks and trailers from the 2nd Battalion, stationed at Seaton, assembled at the Heathfield Camp in Honiton to take the troops, via the Exeter by-pass and Totnes, to take part in this exercise on 17 April 1944. Instructions to personnel *en route* included all British traffic regulations to receive strict compliance, and each vehicle commander would be responsible to see that no object or debris would be thrown from vehicles. The uniform worn was fatigues, with a light pack, steel helmet, gloves and overcoat, and a hot meal was provided upon arrival at the destination. The second Battalion were at Slapton for the purpose of engaging in firing exercises, but it is not known if they took part in the sea operation.

As D-Day approached, the area round East Devon became very active, as American troops were dispersed in country lanes and woods. On the eve of the great day all the troops suddenly disappeared and Seaton seemed a different town; we certainly missed them.

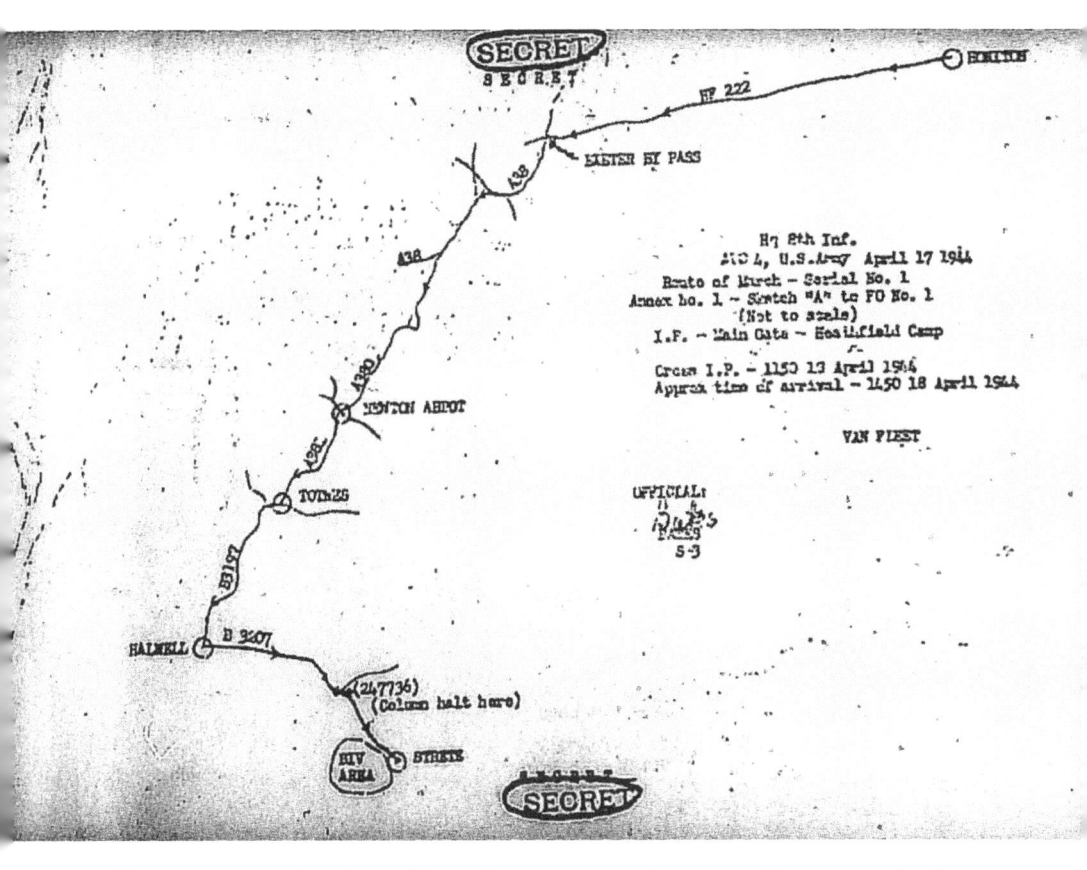

The secret route for the 2nd Battalion to use on the way to Slapton, 17 April 1944.

The 4th Infantry Division embarked on 5 June 1944 from Torbay, on their way to Utah Beach by transport boats. Utah Beach was the code name for the right flank or westernmost of the Allied landing beaches during the D-Day invasion of Normandy as part of Operation Overlord. The landing was planned in four waves. The first consisted of twenty Higgins boats, or LCVPs, each carrying a thirty-man assault team from the 8th Infantry Regiment. Personnel from the 2nd Bn took part, and are listed on two of these boats.

The first American soldier to come ashore on D-Day was Leonard Max Schroeder Jr. (1918–2009). As a captain he commanded Company F of the 2nd Battalion, so he could have been stationed at Seaton. In his boat was Brigadier General Roosevelt, the son of President Theodore Roosevelt.

Although he was fifty-six years old and suffering from heart trouble, he earned the Medal of Honour by leading his men under fire at the landing. One month after landing at Utah Beach he died of a heart attack in France.

EMBARKATION PERSONNEL ROSTER
HIGGINS BOAT NO. 44

Sparks, Albert C.	1st Lt
Wilson, Francis J.	2nd Lt
Conklin, James R.	Cpl
Georgiow, George P.	Pvt
Rudman, Robert G.	Tec 5
Russo, John J.	S Sgt
Schwartz, Nat	S Sgt
Scarlata, Frank C.	Pfc
Besson, Hyppolite J.	Pvt
Bottari, Louis J.	Pvt
Dupras, Phillippe G.	Pvt
Killarney, James	Pvt
Rubarts, Delton C.	Pvt
Philip, Michael W.	Sgt
Jones, David C.	Tec 5
Tash, Abraham	Pfc
Younkin, Paul C.	Pfc
Cason, Lee B.	Pvt
Courtney, William D.	Pvt
Detweiler, John T.	Pvt
Alonso, Manuel R.	Tec 4
Mauldin, Bolen E.	Tec 5
Cerqua, Louis C.	Pfc
Garofone, Edward	Pfc
Burk, Albert	Pvt
Moody, Howard	Pvt
Rolen, Raymond E.	Pvt
Maloney, Thomas	Pfc
Petyone, Peter J.	Pfc

3

Some Personal Recollections of American Soldiers in Seaton and Other Memories of Seaton during the Second World War

Frank Akerman

Although I was only born some three months after the outbreak of war, many of my earliest recollections are of course of wartime Seaton. How many of these memories coincide only with the time during which American soldiers were stationed in Seaton is not certain but, as a family, our contact with two particular servicemen remains very clear, although the photographs below from the family album have undoubtedly helped keep their memory alive.

My father, Bill Akerman, having served in France during the Great War (the war to end all wars!) would certainly have understood just how much the young servicemen stationed in Seaton, from whatever country, would be missing their own homes, families and friends and, as a special constable, he would frequently meet and talk to them on his 'rounds' of the town.

Their visits to us in Jasmine Cottage for meals were a highlight for a four year old, although this maybe had something to do with packets of chewing gum, of which supplies were plentiful! As you can see from the photograph above, they were able to borrow family bicycles and their impressions of Seaton and the surrounding areas, which they sent home to their families, must have been quite special for not only did these relatives send the most marvellous and very welcome food parcels to us for several years (food rationing continued for some years after the end of the war) but also the relatives and possibly the widow/girlfriend of one of them came to visit us in about 1948 or 1949.

Jasmine Cottage is opposite the Pole Arms and the singing echoed down the street every night. In those years all pubs had a piano as part of their standard furniture and I am quite sure the Americans will have joined in: certainly I think it likely that I became very familiar with the American

Left: Sergeant John (Jack) Coggins and Kenneth Austin on bicycles they borrowed on a number of occasions, in the back garden of Jasmine Cottage.

Right: Jasmine Cottage, 1 May 1944. Back row left to right: Sgt. John Coggins, Isobel Akerman, Gladys Akerman, Private Kenneth Austin. The children left to right: Philip Badcock, Frances Akerman, Peter Badcock and Paul Badock. Frank Akerman is seated on the bicycle in front. Sergeant Jack Coggins and Kenneth Austin (both in the 2nd Battalion 8th Infantry Division of the United States Army) were killed in the June D-Day landings. Peter Badcock was killed by the Mau Mau in Kenya when doing his National Service. Frances Akerman died in a car accident in April 1954. Gladys Akerman died in 1979. Paul Badcock died in 2012 after a very distinguished career as an engineer in the Royal Navy.

Some Personal Recollections of American Soldiers in Seaton...

Pictured in the back garden of Jasmine Cottage, Seaton, in May 1944 are, left to right: Isobel Akerman, Bill Akerman, Kenneth Austin, Frank Akerman (on the shoulders), John Coggins, Frances Akerman, Gladys Akerman. Sergeant John Coggins and Kenneth Austin (both in the 2nd Battalion, 8th Infantry Division, United States Army) were killed in the D-day landings on 6 June, within five weeks of this photo being taken.

Left to right: Francis Akerman, Peter Badcock, Isobel Akerman, Paul Badcock. Standing in the rear: Kenneth Austin and John Coggins. In the front of the picture we have Frank Akerman and Philip Badcock.

Left to right: Gladys Akerman, Bill Akerman (bending over) and John Coggins' widow, Blanche who, on a visit to Seaton about three years after the end of the war, went to Branscombe churchyard. Here she was shown the tomb of the Revenue (coastguard) office who died on the cliffs while pursuing smugglers in the early nineteenth century.

folk song, 'Polly Wolly Doodle' at this time. Incidentally, this tradition of community singing went on for many years and well into the 1950s, almost certainly finally killed off by the lack of pianists and the arrival of juke boxes. Pub closing time was often noisy and, as you might expect from a crowd of young testosterone-fuelled youths facing an uncertain future, there were a number of incidents, most of which I suspect went undetected in the pitch blackness of a wartime night, despite the best efforts of the local constabulary.

However, l do remember one night being woken by a family commotion when my father was called out on duty. A lorry heading south from Axmouth with its dimmed lights (blackout restrictions were strictly enforced) had failed to negotiate the tight right hand bend on to the old bridge. The lorry crashed through the barrier, the tide was unfortunately full and I believe three servicemen drowned,
although I am not sure if they were part of the American contingent or came from another national force also stationed in Seaton.

Some Personal Recollections of American Soldiers in Seaton...

Just above the east side of the river mouth there was an emplacement for an anti-aircraft gun: imagine the thrill for a small boy of being allowed to sit on the seat of the gun as it rotated through 360 degrees! Again, this may not have been an American site but, looking back, I am sure the frequent convoys we met on the main roads around Seaton were part of the American and Allied build-up for D-Day: trucks, tanks, jeeps and covered wagons crawled past in a seemingly endless and incredibly noisy line being constantly shepherded by motor-cyclists who made sure that the few other road users waited by the side of the road until they had passed.

Other familiar noises included the quite frequent wail of the siren warning us of approaching aircraft, a signal for everyone to find a place of relative safety. The Badcock family next door to Jasmine Cottage, in their house adjacent to the Central Garage, had a large steel cage called, I believe, a Morrison shelter. My grandparents at 19/21 Fore Street had a 'walk-in' concrete shelter with bunk beds, but very often it was just a matter of scrambling under the dining room table.

Sometimes we would hear the distant drone of passing planes on their way to west country targets such as Exeter, but just occasionally the planes would unload any remaining bombs on their way home and Seaton suffered two such incidents with the sad loss of life: the explosion of the Cliff House bomb, even at some distance, was tremendous and I have a memory of feathers and other debris blowing
up Fore Street. The distant noise of labouring trains as they climbed the Honiton incline west of Seaton junction was also a familiar sound, clearly heard in Seaton when the wind was from the north. In common with the road convoys, huge amounts of military hardware was shifted by rail and, having a grandfather who was keen on trains in general, it was a favoured expedition to Seaton Junction or the level crossing in Axminster to watch this greatly increased rail traffic with seemingly endless lines of open trucks carrying every sort of military vehicle, often pulled by a pair of huge engines which pounded past in a flurry of steam and sparks.

I am not sure when half of a huge landing craft was washed up on the shore just below the old Beach Hotel. Exactly how it had sustained its broken back was certainly unknown then but my particular memory is of walking past the wreck when the stores were being emptied and the sailors involved (Americans?) were tossing tins of what must have seemed to be exotic food to local people on the beach. As a result of this chance encounter I remember tasting tinned grapefruit for the first time!

The radio was seldom switched off and news bulletins were frequent but I cannot specifically remember D-Day nor do I know when and how we first found out that both Kenneth and John had been killed, but I think it was some weeks later. I do know that their deaths made a deep impression on our family (my sisters at the time were fifteen and twelve) and brought home the real tragedy of war.

Our debt to these two young American soldiers and to all their fellow servicemen is incalculable: the war in Europe will surely have seemed very distant to these two young men, one from St. Petersburg in Florida and the other from Baltimore and yet they willingly came to defend and in the end to die for a cause which may well have seemed obscure and possibly even somewhat irrelevant to them.

The generations born during and since the Second World War I hope will always remember the ultimate sacrifice made by young men like Kenneth Austin and John Coggins: their lasting contribution to the life of so many of us has been the maintenance of relative peace and prosperity during the last seven decades.

Clive Boyce

My recollections of the war period in Seaton are very limited and especially of the American Forces. All that I can recall of US troops is that we used to hover around the camp between the Old and New Beer Roads (very near Check House) and cadge sweets and of course ask 'got any gum chum?' I also remember the occasion when a jeep returning to Seaton from Axmouth (probably from a visit to the Harbour Inn) failed to negotiate the right turn onto the bridge and went straight into the river. I believe the consequences were tragic.

Just before D-Day I saw hundreds of US troops around the 'Radio Location Station' on the Seaton-Sidmouth Road where I suspect they were billeted. Clearly something was pending. Beryl Badcock, mother of my best friend Peter, used to socialise with the US troops a lot. Philip might remember a few details.

My father, Leicester Boyce, had gone to the bank and was returning and had reached Burnham's. I was on the other side of the road on the corner of Station Road. Whilst I had been waiting I had noticed a plane high in the sky with its engines droning. I suddenly saw several objects leave the plane and I called out, 'Dad what's that?' He picked me up, hurled us through our shop door and lay on me. Immediately the loudest bang you could imagine hit us, followed by dust and all manner of fragments of building material. When the dust had settled we saw there had been a

Some Personal Recollections of American Soldiers in Seaton...

direct hit on the end house on Castle Hill. The Square was deep in bomb debris. Windows everywhere in the vicinity were broken and roof slates shattered. I understood about five people in the house were killed and that one of them was in the WRENS and was going to return to base later that day. Checking it looks as though it was the Cartwright family. I am not sure about the name.

I see on PreeBMD there were two Cartwright deaths, John R. aged sixty and Isabella aged fifty-eight registered Honiton in December 1942. The event must have been before October 1943 as my father was killed on active service at that time.

We used to attend the parish church regularly and one Sunday I remember Revd Cook appealing to the congregation to go straight after the service to the beach with buckets and spades. The objective was to dig an enormous ditch which would prevent German tanks from crossing the beach. I remember Revd Cook brewing up tea in the boot of his car to encourage the residents to keep digging. Clearly we made very little impact on the beach and the next high tide ensured no impact at all. This was of course before all the ironwork adorned the beach.

Once, Peter Badcock and I were playing in our yard at the Esplanade. I am not sure the air raid warning sounded (if it had I am sure we would have run indoors). Suddenly a German plane flew very low over our heads and we were peppered with machine gun bullets (or similar). We both escaped injury but the corrugated iron roofs above were full of holes. I suspect it was a very narrow escape. Someone else was less scared than us as when we went out into Station Road one of our bikes had been pinched. We thought about it charitably and assumed someone wanted to make a quick get away to safety.

The 2nd Battalion of Czech Army was stationed in Seaton and I remember my father giving some of them the run of his bakery. I think some were billeted in what had been the Esplanade Hotel. Our reward was some very special poppy seed bread. I seem to remember the Czechs being very kind to us and giving my sister Wendy and I presents. I am convinced I remember Edvard Beneš, President of the Czech Government in exile, visiting Seaton. I also recollect an amazing military funeral with Czech military looking resplendent. I think a couple of their number had been killed somewhere in the vicinity of the landslip. The story was they had stepped on a mine.

Jean Claridge

I was evacuated from Birmingham to my grandmother in Seaton. Mrs Alice Claridge was housekeeper to Mr Richard Hudson of Baunkyle, Bunts Lane, Seaton, a Birmingham businessman, Baunkyle being his country home. I was in Seaton for the duration of the war, only returning to Birmingham for a few months when my father thought that the Germans would soon be landing on the south coast. During my time in Birmingham (1941) our house was bombed and so I returned to Seaton. I attended Chine School, Manor House and Colyton Grammar.

Mr Hudson had two small boats at Beer and was allowed a petrol ration so that we could catch fish. He also had two ' shoots' so that we had our own supply of game. When we had more fish than we could eat I was sent out, usually with Jean, to deliver some to the neighbours, amongst these were the Misses Grinsell who lived in Durley Road, and the Goddards who lived at the top of Bunts Lane. Because of the war Mr. Hudson's chauffer/gardener, Mr Cecil Collier, of Beer, was sent to work part-time at the Goddards', to save manpower.

Because I was an evacuee people were very kind to me and I remember Maud Richards at the brickyard's cottages where I used to go for tea and, of course, Mr and Mrs Litton were particularly kind and Jean's home was my second home. Mrs Stentiford, Margaret's mother also made me very welcome. Mrs Stentiford always seemed busy working for the war effort. I remember her making camouflage nets etc in her living room. There was a very sad incident when two little evacuees, Stella and June, and Mr and Mrs Eels were killed, but I know that Jean has written a separate article about this.

One of my first memories was of the sinking of HMS *Courageous*, by a German U-boat in the south western approaches (south west of Ireland). This occurred on 17 September 1939. The captain was W. T. Makeig Jones and of course the Makeig Jones family lived in Fremington Road. I was very impressed as a small girl to be told that Captain Makeig Jones stood on the bridge of his ship saluting until the ship went down and he with it. This may be apocryphal, but I have always remembered it.

There was an incident when we were at Chine School, on a rather rough and blustery day, when we saw a plane fly in, nearly reaching the shore, when it 'ditched' in the sea. Presumably it was one of 'ours' but I never knew whether the crew managed to get out safely.

Peace was declared on 8 May 1945, and I was at the cinema in Seaton with Jean watching *The Story of Dr. Wassell* starring Gary Cooper and

Laraine Day. The film was interrupted by, I think, an announcement that Mr. Churchill was speaking to say that the war in Europe had finished. The whole cinema erupted in shouts and cheering.

Georgia Miller, née Peach

It must have been my brother, Albert, who first became friendly with the American soldiers, as he was seven years older than myself. My parents, Jack and Doll Peach, issued an invitation to a trio of soldiers to experience Seaton's hospitality. One of these kept in contact with our family when war was over. His name was Don Jones, from Cadiz, Ohio. We received food parcels from him containing rich fruit ring cakes decorated with crystallised fruit and nuts, jelly in crystal form (we only knew the blocks of jelly) and, of course, chewing gum.

As time went on we lost contact with each other until, out of the blue, our postman, Len Northcott, delivered a letter to my mother, who now lived in Elmfield Road. The address on the envelope was Mr & Mrs J. Peach, 1 Highwell. As postmen do in our area, he knew exactly who the letter was for, and where they now lived. Sadly by now my father had died, but Don was coming to England and wrote that he would love to see us all.

Mum answered straight away, saying that we would love to see him, and he was welcome to stay with her. Once again we were able to show him our hospitality, and show him how Seaton had altered. Sadly, soon after returning to America his daughter informed us that he had died.

Photo taken in Highwell Road, where we were living, of 'Baby' to the left, Joe to the right, and the ragamuffin in the middle, myself. Mrs Miller is in the centre. Joe left behind his Bible for my brother, but was sadly killed whilst fighting. 'Baby' remained friends with Don.

Some Personal Recollections of American Soldiers in Seaton...

Don on the ground where the American billets were built on Station Road, now Harbour Road opposite the holiday camp. Norcombe Court is now where Don is standing.

A view of Don's house.

MEMORIES OF US SERVICEMEN IN SEATON IN 1944

Sandy Grant

For most of the war, my mother lived with us, her three children, at a house which was then called Floof (flat roof) on the New Beer Road. My father, at the time, must have been with the 8th Army in Italy. At the bottom of the hill there was a US army base squeezed into the fork of the New and Old Beer Roads. Today, that area is replete with housing and there is nothing to suggest that an army base ever existed there.

In 1944, I was aged eight. Every time I went into town and back, I may have made a habit of stopping at the entrance to the base to chat up the poor soul on guard duty. I wasn't being deliberately friendly—I was most certainly on a hunt for chewing gum.

My mother did her best to befriend the US army people, to invite them when they were off duty and to make them feel at home. I have no idea how many came to the house, how often they came or what they did when they were there. There was of course no television and people then had different ways of entertaining themselves. I imagine that my mother's principal intention was to get them out of the base into a home where they could relax, where there were children, enjoy the place, its garden and its lovely view of the sea. Presumably, there were meals—my mother turned herself into a very capable cook—and doubtless would have welcomed the normally unavailable goodies, such as ice cream, that her American guests were able to contribute.

My own recollections of those visits are limited but remain vivid. I know that I was particularly friendly with several of those service men—whose names I have long lost. I remember them talking about their homes—places with exotic sounding names like Idaho, and Illinois, California and Kansas. I have a vague idea that they made me promise that one day I would visit all of those places. Perhaps that notion was related to our conversations, which, on my part, dwelt on the foodstuffs such as bananas, which I knew about but had never seen, or more importantly, tasted. Perhaps they suggested that when I got to America I would have as many bananas as I could possibly want. Perhaps they thought that I could be a surrogate for themselves just in case...

My notion that they were desperately homesick could only have survived all the subsequent years because they themselves told me as much. During these visits there must have been the good times with much fun and laughter—but perhaps these were adult jollities in which a young child would have had no place.

My recollection is of a bunch of people who were incredibly good to me—but who had a sadness about them which has remained etched in my memory. In particular I have one face in mind—someone who had been especially kind to me perhaps, who seems to be gazing intently into the distance. At the time, I knew nothing of D-Day which must then have been imminent, so that this could not be an example of memory induced by the subsequent passage of time. But I do suggest that what I then regarded as sadness was in fact, apprehension—something that I would not have been able to recognise at that time.

I have long wondered what might have happened to our friends. I presume that they took part in the cross Channel invasion and I also presume that some of them never made it home. There must, however, be a record of the fate of those who belonged to that particular unit.

It has annoyed me for many years now that there is still no plaque to indicate that this was once a US army base. May I suggest that this is the moment to correct that omission. A plaque should provide details of the units that were stationed there and for what period of time. It should also state when the base was closed down and the buildings demolished. I also feel that the plaque should express gratitude to the men who were stationed there and especially to those who later died in France and Germany in order that others, not least in Seaton, could live in freedom.

Len Northcott

My main contact with our visitors was through the Doughnut Dugout, their equivalent to our NAAFI. This was two flats knocked into one, now above Frydays. When we delivered Telegrams there we were always offered coffee and doughnuts, and what boy was going to refuse? Sometimes we might go two or three times a day, then miss two or three.

One memory that sticks in my mind is looking out the window onto the car park jammed full of Jeeps and lorries and seeing the GIs playing cards on the canvas backs of the Jeeps. If they had no change they would tear a ten-shilling note or a £1 note in half and I often wondered how many notes got back together.

At this time I was wearing three stripes on my right arm, bright red on navy blue. These were only for good conduct, but a lot of the young privates would insist on calling you sir, even though I was only a couple of years younger than most of them.

With reference to Georgina Miller's report and the photo of Don Jones, he is standing in front of the old Labour Exchange. This area was before the war Warner's Holiday Camp Amusement Park.
Looking from Harbour Road South on the left was a purpose building for bumper cars, this was converted into workshops and on the right a similar one housing slot machines and stalls, this was converted into billets.

INFORMATION ON SEATON DEFENCES

Ron Anning

Along the whole of the beach from Seaton Hole to the River Axe, approximately twelve feet high, of iron scaffolding was erected.
The West Walk area, the Cliff top, putting green, and three shelters, were surrounded with barbed wire and were taken over by the Royal Artillery. The shelters became Guardrooms.

Two searchlight positions were built on the West Walk—one is still there today, the other one was on the left hand side of the Chine Café. I believe it is still there, grown over on Check House land.

On the top of the cliff were mounted two six-inch naval guns. A few of the local Home Guard were trained by the Royal Artillery to fire them. I was a member and we used to practice on Sunday morning.

On the East Walk three pillboxes were built, one at the top of Trevelyan Road, one on Beach Road (machine gun position), and the Gap and the roundabout by Midland Bank. R. G. Spiller of Chard were responsible for building the pillboxes. Herman Anning Ron and Len's father was employed by R. G. Spiller.

There was one air raid shelter by the new Post Office and the River Axe was dammed with lines of cement barges below the bridge.

June Richards, née Sweetland

June Sweetland was an Axmouth girl

I was six when the war started and can remember all the grief from the older ones. My Gran who lived next to us was very upset because it meant that her other four sons would be going to war. The two eldest had served in the last war and were invalided out. You can imagine what my Granny was feeling like now. She died within a few months of the start of the war, 3 September 1939. She was taken by 'The Big C' and I remember thinking that I did not like The Big C, whoever *he* was.

We carried on with raising money for the war effort, mending mosquito nets, knitting string vests and growing our own vegetables and fruit etc. I remember one day they took the iron railings from the bottom of our front garden. The day came when my Dad came home from work and declared he had invited six American lads from overseas to have a meal with us. It was lovely and we did enjoy seeing them. In time, they visited us quite regularly and became part of the family. They helped out with the garden and feeding the pigs and poultry etc. They even taught my Dad to grow tobacco plants and make his own tobacco.

We loved having the lads with us and we enjoyed many a happy meal. As Christmas was coming we realised we would have twenty-two for dinner with us so it was decided we would have to kill another goose. This one had four wings. There being so many, the children had their meal first, then the grown-ups. We went into the other room and were listening for comments as my Dad carved up the goose with four wings. It was with great delight we heard the comments.

After that one by one my uncles came home to see us. My Mum asked, 'Is this IT?' whatever *it* was. We soon realised that something was going on. We were expecting our American soldiers to arrive for Sunday lunch, but they were late, so we thought that *it* had arrived, and my Mum and Dad looked decidedly unhappy. The next thing we heard was the sound of the jeep and in walked Big Mac, Little Mac, Leon, Tex, Charles and Lucerne, carrying a large can and another even larger can. They contained ice cream and peaches! We had never tasted them before and they were lovely. The peaches lasted most of the week.

Suddenly they didn't come anymore and we thought they had gone back overseas and we would hear from them later on. We never did hear from any of them again.

Years later we heard all about the Americans lost when they were rehearsing in the Channel and were torpedoed by a German Submarine. We wondered if that was why we never heard from any of them again. Happily my Mother's six brothers all came home, two of them the worse for wear and died partly because of their wounds several years later.

SECOND WORLD WAR SEATON MEMORIES

Tony Burges

The Beach, Seafront and the Axe Valley Defences
The entire beach had 20- to 30-foot high metal pole barricades with three lines of concrete drums covered with barbed wire. However, there was a gap in these defences for the fishing boats to go to sea at Fishermen's Gap.

There were two searchlight structures along the West Walk (one still exists) to light the bay should there be a night attack, to assist the two naval guns mounted on Cliff Field above. These were manned by regular troops supported by the Home Guard. Every Sunday morning the two naval guns would have firing practice as a fast naval launch would tow a target across the bay. The gunfire would shake shop windows and be some entertainment for the public.

Sunday mornings were important to the Home Guard (Dad's Army) as it was drill and field exercises, with 303 rifles and blank cartridges, and Bren guns with fire crackers as ammunition. Live ammunition was not issued to the Home Guard in the early years of the war, as it was scarce. It was amusing to watch the Home Guard, at noon on Sundays after their training they would dismiss and all end up in the George Inn—but they would leave their 303 rifles neatly stacked outside the pub—perhaps Jerry doesn't invade on Sundays.

There were defences in place, a pillbox on Castle Hill, an anti-aircraft gun at the top of Trevelyan Road, a circular pillbox in the Square opposite Lloyds Bank, camouflaged as a café with a pink roof, and concrete water tanks in Seafield Gardens and in Queen Street, for firefighting. There were also large concrete barricades at the bottom Fore Street and Eyre Court Road. A public air raid shelter was built in the Grove (where I sheltered with my parents on many a night) and another in Queen Street. The air raid siren was mounted on the Fire Station tower in Harepath Road, now a retail store.

There were volunteer Police Specials and Air Raid Wardens on duty throughout the war, with the Police Station at the top of Eyre Court Road. Often you would hear a shout at night, 'put that light out!' as a warden on patrol would discover a house with a glint of light showing behind curtains. Many buildings had sticky brown paper crossed on windows to prevent bomb blast shatter. One morning we found the entire Seaton marshes covered with silver paper strips about 18 inches long, which had been dropped by the RAF in order to disrupt the German radar.

Early in the war the Seaton Marshes, the cliff tops, and the Golf Course area were covered with thousands of 15 foot wooden posts erected some 100 yards apart. This was to cause damage to invading German troop-carrying glider aircraft as they landed.

The Taunton Stop Line

This line ran some 50 miles with a variety of defences to delay a German advance from the West. It ran from the mouth of the River Axe via Taunton to Highbridge. Heavy machine gun pillboxes and anti-tank gun emplacements were camouflaged as hayricks, cottages and cafés.

With so many defensive obstacles at Seaton and the Axe Valley it seems we were ripe for a German invasion. I clearly remember the false hayrick with its pillbox inside at Bosshill Cross and the false cafe on the Axmouth Road. There are several hundred of these defences still visible today along the route, no doubt there would have been a considerable battle here in the west if the Germans had advanced.

German Bombing and Other Incidents

Land mines were buried on Axe Cliff, where some Czech soldiers were tragically killed, also a lady walking her dog.

It was a Thursday lunchtime when I heard the air raid siren, so I took cover under my bed in 10 Marine Place, Seaton. Then there was a blast as a German bomb had dropped on the Cartwrights' house, now the Festival Gardens, killing a Wren on leave and the family in the house. The debris from the bomb landed on our house, where we had just repaired the last of the bomb damaged roof. Another German bomb was dropped in Highwell Road, with a direct hit killing several evacuees. A further German bomb was dropped on a house at the bottom of Townsend Road, which shattered our nursery of greenhouses with tomatoes growing, belonging to my Aunt and Uncle. This was a business started by my grandfather in the 1800s and sadly never recovered from the enemy damage.

Mrs Walton, the wife of the Seaton St Gregory's Parish Church organist, was machine gunned and killed on 12 August 1942 by a German aircraft as she walked down Townsend Road. Towards the latter part of the war two German prisoners escaped from a working party at Dymonds Farm, Clyst Honiton. They found their way to Axmouth Harbour where they stole a boat and some provisions. They rowed out and came ashore below the Undercliff. Here they were successful in finding shelter and living off the land, stealing food and provisions, some probably from Dowlands Farm, Rousdon. At night they took water from the well at Annie Gapper's cottage nearby. It was several weeks before they were recaptured.

Food and Health

A boiled egg was something of a luxury, meat and butter (2 ozs. only per week) were rationed. Rabbits were plentiful so you would net, shoot or snare with ferrets and dogs. Fresh fish were not always available but salted fish was. Saccharines were a substitute for sugar. There was no butter and no cream but milk came from Ern Harris, who delivered by horse and cart. We had no bananas or any imported fruit, but on a Sunday we could occasionally have a chicken dinner. Only at Christmas, perhaps, we had a goose from the smallholding of Mr Ben Welsh in Station Road. An orange in your Christmas stocking was a wonderful treat.

Towards the end of the war imported apples in wooden barrels arrived, and clothing from Canada—we all looked like little lumberjacks. The WVS operated a canteen in the Burrow for the large number of troops in Seaton. We lads found it great as the American troops gave chewing gum and doughnuts to us. This was something new and special.

Transport

Transport was restricted as there was fuel rationing, but with the railway we were more fortunate than others. Each Saturday a goods wagon would be loaded at Seaton Station with freshly killed rabbits for London. The Southern National bus service kept running, but fuel for business cars was rationed, with travel restrictions.

Troops in the Area

British, USA, Polish, Czechs and others were stationed in Seaton. There was a barracks alongside the New Beer Road, and parades through Seaton on Sundays.

There were military vehicle depots in Station Road, at Trevetts car park and on land opposite the Holiday Camp. This preparation was all prior to the Normandy invasion.

The American Troops would regularly play baseball at the cricket field.

Malvern House School for Girls was evacuated from Lewisham during the Second World War; this group photograph was taken c. 1942. They were housed in the Manor House at Seaton, and it was at this time that the name was changed to the Manor House School.

The War Effort
Camouflage nets for tanks, guns etc. were made at the Beach Hotel garage. Many women knitted gloves and jumpers for the troops.

During the war metal gates and railings were cut away from premises, the metal was used to build tanks and ships etc. Some of the metal stumps can still be seen. I remember the railings being cut at Manor House School and at Netherhayes.

The Vicar
At the Vicarage there was a First Aid Post ably run by the ever popular Reverend Cooke, who kept everyone's spirits up as he came into town each day with his enthusiasm and a greeting—he was such a great character to have around in wartime.

Children

We children had to pick rose hips along the Colyford Road in the Black Pool Field, for the making of Rose Hip Syrup as a source of Vitamin C. Many were under-nourished with the shortage of food, so in Britain children were given one third of a pint of milk free at school. Cod liver oil and orange drinks were also allocated to help the nutrition of the children.

Wilf Collins

In 1944 I was fifteen going on sixteen, and had just started an apprenticeship with the local gas company. Our workshops were, at that time, behind the Town Hall. One of my colleagues was a regular user of the George Inn in the Square, where he got to know a few of the American soldiers who were in the town at that time. He would turn up at work with cartons of Lucky Strike, Philip Morris, Chesterfield and Camel cigarettes, in packs of 200—sometimes cigars as well.

This led to him bringing spent cannon shell cases, to which we soldered the old bronze 3*d* pieces, as souvenirs to be sent to the USA by the GIs, who were taken by the coin.

I got to know a sergeant, who was a cook based in the old holiday camp, and on my way home one night, after having done a soldering job for him, I went into the camp to give him the shells. I was invited to have dinner with him, and we sat down together in the dining room. We had a wonderful roast dinner, but to my surprise there was a dollop of jam on the plate—very unusual. I have often wondered if any of the souvenirs reached America, and if any of the relatives still have them.

Who remembers Donut Dugout, that was in one of the buildings in the Burrow? Lovely ring donuts, a real treat.

The hospital that was built at Millwey Rise in Axminster led to the GIs coming down through the villages looking for booze, especially whisky, which was in very short supply. They were in the habit of using one of their ambulances for this, and one evening, after passing through Axmouth, they failed to negotiate the rather sharp right-hand bend at the end of the Waterside road to go over the old Axmouth Bridge, and ended up in the river. Unfortunately three men were drowned in the accident.

Another thing that was peculiar at the time was that the GIs wore rubber-soled boots. We were accustomed to the crisp sound of the hobnail boots when our troops were on the march, but the Americans were silent in their approach. Instead of the left, right, left, right of the

British commands, the American command was hup two, three, four—very strange to my ears.

Thelma Critchard

The Secret

Walking along the Front at Seaton recently, on a rare bright sunny afternoon, with families sitting on the beach enjoying picnics and children frolicking in the sea, I was reminded of the long hot summer of 1945, just before the end of the war.

My Father was in the Home Guard and, although we lived in Axminster, one of his duties on Saturdays and Sundays was to cycle to Seaton to check the rather grandly named 'Sea Defences' which consisted of huge rolls of barbed wire, spread along the beach just above the high water mark. This was presumably to halt an imminent German invasion. There was no access to the Front, much to the dismay of local families and all the properties along there were boarded up.

If the weather was fine, my Father would take me in a child's seat on the back of his cycle. Pedalling all the way on a big iron bicycle, in full heavy Home Guard uniform, must have been quite an effort. Especially as we had to take his bag of tools and our lunch as well!

On arrival he would park up and we would walk slowly along the top of the beach, whilst he inspected the wire for any damage and make repairs if necessary. I could hardly wait until we got to the far end where there was a small gap between the rocks and here we would scramble down to the shore, where we had our sandwiches and I was allowed to take off my shoes and socks and paddle in the rock pools. Oh—joy of joy—such pleasure cannot be described as the waves brought in the icy water over my toes.

All too soon we had to make our way back—me too tired to walk, probably getting a ride on Father's shoulders. No mention of this wonderful adventure was ever made to anyone, not even my Mother, and has remained our secret—until now!

SECOND WORLD WAR GRAVES IN SEATON CHURCHYARD

Joyce Colman

The best-known Second World War graves are probably the two on the left-hand side of the path leading from the Church to the Hall. The two Czech soldiers, Vojtech Drazka and Frant Rocek, were killed together by the explosion of a mine in the Landslip in 1942.

Corporal J. P. Mahoney of the Pioneer Corps was killed in 1944 when an army lorry went over Axe Bridge.

Three other fatalities of the Second World War buried here are:
1) A. G. Newton, a Pilot Officer in the RAF, killed accidentally in Scotland in 1939.
2) Sergeant T. H. Clapp, RAFVR, killed in 1943 on active service over Lincolnshire.
3) Sapper P. E. Harris, killed in 1943 after an accident in Scotland while serving with the Royal Engineers.

There was also a German airman, G. G. Hartung, whose body was recovered from the sea after his plane crashed at Beer. He was buried with full military honours by the RAF but in 1963 his body was exhumed under licence from the Home Office, and reburied in the German Military Burial Ground at Cannock Chase, Staffordshire.

Although this area was considered reasonably safe from air raids, the Registers show that in August 1942 five civilians were killed by a direct hit on 16 Highwell Road: John Paul Eeles and Mary Eeles in Grave 236; Susan Moore (eleven years) and Stella June Moore (six years), who were evacuees, in Grave 291; Elizabeth J. Woolacott, who actually lived in Townsend Road but was visiting the family, in Grave 294; M. G. E. Smith, Grave 123, G. L. Dowse, Grave 404 and Joan Walton, Grave 179, were killed in the same raid.

In October 1942 Lt-Col. John Rogers Cartwright DSO, of the Devonshire Regiment, and his wife Isabella were killed by enemy action in their home, Grave 403. Florence Mary Sercombe, aged fifty-nine, who had been with the family for thirty-one years, was also killed, Grave 34. Mrs Cartwright's mother, Eleanor Jane Pamela Ross, aged eighty-nine, also died, Grave 289.

Some Personal Recollections of American Soldiers in Seaton...

SCOUTS AWARDED THE GILT CROSS FOR GALLANTRY

In August 1943, a twelve-year-old evacuee called Connie Wall was paddling in the River Axe opposite the Axe Cliff Golf Links hill, when she was swept off her feet into the middle of the river. Scouts Ron Anning and Patrol Leader Bill Green were getting dressed having had a swim, when a lady on the path screamed out that a girl was drowning. They immediately swam to her, but by the time they reached her she had gone under twice. Ron managed to grab her by her hair and he and Bill pulled her towards the lady, who had waded in up to her waist and helped them bring her to safety. Connie was taken to Exeter Hospital, where she recovered from her ordeal.

Many years later Connie returned to Seaton and called on Ron to thank him and Bill for saving her life. Unfortunately, all of the family were out, but she spoke to a neighbour.

Ron Anning and Bill Green were presented with the Scout Gilt Cross for Gallantry.

Troop Leader Ronald Anning, left, and Patrol Leader William Green, August 1943. They are wearing their Scout Gilt Crosses, which were presented to them for gallantry by Colonel O'Donnell, the assistant County Commissioner, at a ceremony in the Church Institute, Seaton.

MEMOIRS OF A SEATON TREVELYAN SCHOOL PUPIL

Jean Perkins née Hooper

From September 1939 our wartime education was shared with evacuees from London. There were so many children billeted in the town that our school was not large enough to accommodate us all.

Consequently alternative arrangements were made whereby some pupils were taught in the upstairs areas of the Sunday school at the old Congregational Church (now known as The United Reformed Church).

Each group was housed in curtained off cubicles containing one large table and long forms seating approximately ten pupils. When the siren sounded at the onset of an air raid we were all marched in crocodile from the Church Hall in Cross Street to the rear entrance of the old Regal Cinema, exactly opposite, and up into the foyer where the strengthened ceiling was considered safer for us to shelter until the 'all clear' was sounded and we were able to return to normal classes.

We still managed to learn our 'Three Rs' despite time off for potato picking. As that was just a slight disruption to our young lives, I think we were very fortunate, although the city children may not have felt so lucky having been taken away from their homes and families.

In the days of pre-supermarket Seaton, and all East Devon towns, enjoyed a large number of small shopkeepers, who were able to cope when food rationing began in January 1940, starting with butter, sugar and bacon, but soon extended to include a large number of basic foodstuffs. Everyone was issued with a ration book of coupons entitling them to what nutritionists had calculated was an adequate portion of each rationed item per week. No obese people in those days, and no need for diet plans.

Rationed items could only be bought at a controlled price from shops with which you were registered, and my mother registered at Trumps in Fore Street.

In June 1941 clothes rationing was introduced. The clothes on sale were utility items, unfussy styles and sometimes rather drab.

Photographic surveys of the ancient Parish Churches of Seaton and Axmouth were made during the War, and two copies were kept in separate places so that if the church was destroyed by enemy action, a detailed record on the church might be preserved.

Some Personal Recollections of American Soldiers in Seaton...

Memories—Derek Stephens

The skies around Seaton and East Devon were always busy during the Second World War, and every schoolboy was able to recognise different aircraft. Spitfires and Hurricanes and other fighter planes were easy to spot, and American Liberators from Dunkeswell were often seen.

On Saturday 17 October 1942, ninety-four Lancaster bombers flew over the Axe Valley on the way to a daylight-bombing raid to France. The target was the Schneider works at Le Creusot, a French armament factory. When they passed over the Axe Valley the following memories were recorded.

The late Fred Spiller, a farmer, recalled that as they flew over the copse at the top of Bosshill, 'the trees had to bow down to the ground to let them get by'. A field away Ira Pigeon of Axmouth had severe problems with his wagon horses, and the late Frank Webber of Compyne reckoned he could have reached up and touched the underside of a fuselage with his pitchfork as he stood on the back of his cart. Old farmer Newbury lost a bullock which broke its neck as cattle stampeded into a ditch. Having no tractor, he asked neighbour Fred Spiller if he could bring his tractor to haul the carcass away. Fred suggested he should apply to the authorities for compensation. A little affronted by the suggestion, farmer Newbury replied:

> 'Compensation? Compensation? I don't want no compensation. As long as they go and give old Jerry what for they can keep their compensation!'

Perhaps the wisest reaction to the experience was by retired Seaton postman Gilbey Hutchings who, being a schoolboy at the time, recalled that when he found himself in the centre of a low-flying Armada, he followed school instructions. 'I jumped into a hedge and bide there till they went on'.

NOT THE GLORIOUS TWELFTH

Seaton Vicarage (now flats in Case Gardens) was a Red Cross Post manned by Devon Red Cross Unit 110, with Mrs Cooke, a VAD, and Revd H. R. Cooke, the Chief Air Raid Warden. The downstairs room on the north side was equipped as a two-bedded hospital ward. When the bomb fell on Townsend Road on 12 August 1942, Mrs Walton, wife of William Walton, St Gregory's Church organist, was walking down the road where they lived in Kew Cottage. She was machine-gunned and hit by a tracer bullet along her spine. She was taken to the Vicarage First Aid Post, which must have been a great shock to the vicar and his wife. Sadly, she died the next day. Mr and Mrs Pike, who lived in nearby Harepath Road were injured.

Ron Anning, who was walking home from Ben Turner's building yard, just opposite Seaton Vicarage for his lunch break, had to report to the Vicarage for his scout messenger duties. Many houses were badly damaged, including Manor Cottages and Andy Bartlett's Nursery Garden at the bottom of Townsend Road. The blast blew all the glass out of the greenhouses, which were full of ripening tomatoes. Strangely, some of the glass was blown skywards and the plants were left standing with fruit undamaged. Most of the glass, however, blew inwards and pounds of tomatoes were covered in splintered glass—a real loss in times of rationing. The greenhouses were repaired by Andy Bartlett, Ted Gosling and Bill Smith while Ben Turner and his employees (including Ron Anning) were kept busy with surrounding properties.

A LUCKY ESCAPE

Jean Cozens née Litton

On 12 August 1942, a bomb fell on 16 Highwell Road, Seaton, killing John and May Eeles, two evacuees, Stella Moore, aged eleven and June Moore, aged six, who were living with them, and Elisabeth Woolacott, who was visiting. The children's mother had been on a visit two weeks earlier and the children had begged to return to London with her, as they were homesick. Sadly, they were due to go home shortly after they were killed.

On that fateful day I was due to go to play and have tea at number 16. My father was Manager at SWEB and we lived in the flat above. On that afternoon at the rear of the premises a load of builder's sand was delivered. My friend Jean Claridge, who had been sent to stay with her grandmother in Bunts Lane to avoid the bombing raids in Birmingham, and I were having a lovely time making sandcastles, and time sped by. My mother called me to tell me to hurry up, as I was late going to Highwell Road. Just at that moment there was a terrific bomb blast, and the rest you know. I remember the ladies from the hairdressers, Lorelei, next door to us, all rushed out into the road with curlers in their hair. Later that evening a policeman came to the flat and showed me a ring with a Devon pixie on it. He asked me if I'd seen it before—I had, it was Stella's.

Some Personal Recollections of American Soldiers in Seaton...

This rare and remarkable photograph show the bomb damage on 16 Highwell Road, 12 August 1942. My friend Seymour Martin and his parents lived in an adjoining house, which was also demolished, but the Martin family escaped.

I will always be grateful to whoever ordered that sand—but for that, I should not be writing this.

A SOLE SURVIVOR IN SEAFIELD HOUSE

On 26 October 1942, at 1.20 p.m., a bomb fell on Seafield House, Seahill, Seaton, now the site of Jubilee Gardens. The house was completely demolished and the vicar, Revd H. R. Cooke, Chief Air Raid Warden, and many helpers, worked long and hard to dig out any survivors. Major Cartwright, DSO, his wife Isabella and her mother Mrs Ross were all killed. However, a nurse, M. G. E. Smith, who was looking after Mrs Ross, survived—as did a corgi dog. Miss Muriel Hawker, aged fourteen (now Mrs Turl of Colyton) was dug out alive from under the kitchen table and was taken to Homestead Nursing Home, The Esplanade, manned by the local Red Cross.

There is a wooden memorial tablet to the Wren in Membury Parish Church.

> In loving memory of Leading Wren Dorothy Downes Wilkin, born 30 November 1920 at Yarty House in this Parish. Killed by enemy action at Seaton, 26 October 1942.

There is also a Service Headstone in the churchyard.

D. D. Wilkin, Leading Wren 7459, Women's Royal Naval Service. 26 October 1942, aged 21. Killed by enemy action at Seaton, Devon.

4
Those Who Served

John Cochrane

John was at college in the RAF and was a radio operator. He was very keen on flying, although he had bad eyesight. In 1941 Germans invaded Russia, so no operators were needed. He therefore trained as a pilot and he would ferry aeroplanes to places.

John learnt with the ATA training school and at the end of the war he worked with the ATA. John was at school in Ireland when the war broke out. He joined up in 1942 and went to a college in Cambridge. John was well informed about the war, as he listened to the radio and comedy shows.

He was worried about German invasions and at school they had a whistle and when it was blown they would all panic and get guns and rifles. When the war ended he was dispersed to different airfields and he took part in celebrations. As he was in London helping look after the aircraft displays he took lots of photos of London.

John lost two cousins, one in the navy who was blown up in the Mediterranean Sea and one in artillery who was shot.

John thought that the war was an adventure as he was given a Spitfire and he was rather disappointed when it ended. In the ATA there were a lot of pilots.

His parents were in Ireland and his mother ran the Red Cross, they would go into the mountains to gather moss for wound dressings.

John missed fresh fruit such as bananas when he was in the army, and when the war ended he was very sorry to leave as he had made a lot of new friends. He also did not want to leave the aeroplanes.

Above left: Chief Petty Officer Arthur James Chapple HSD, RNR, *c.* 1943. Born in 1915, Arthur Chapple was the third son of a Beer fisherman, and like all boys of that village was born for the sea. He left school to become a fisherman on the Arctic trawler fleet. He mobilized in 1939 and served on the Western Ocean convoys and Canadian new constructions. He transferred to general service in 1946, and served in the West Indies, the South Atlantic, Antarctica, the Mediterranean and the Far East. He retired from the Navy in 1961.

Above right: Des Garret, pictured in 1944, had a varied career during the Second World War. He joined the Home Guard at the age of seventeen and later transferred to the Royal Artillery where he trained on the 6-inch naval guns mounted on the cliffs above Seaton's West Walk. He later joined the Royal Navy, serving on the aircraft carrier HMS *Furious* with the Home Fleet at Scapa Flow and then transferring to HMS *Milford* at Portland. Des then retrained as a transport driver for the East Indies and was in the landing party at Port Dickson, Malaya. Father of Seaton Town Council, he was one of the town's most popular personalities.

Seaman Reginald Thomas ('Rex') Good RNRP/X7734 of Cliff Hotel, Seaton, who died of wounds received in action on 11 April 1941. Rex was serving on SS *Draco* when she was attacked by divebombers at Tobruk on 11 April 1941. Mortally wounded with severe leg wounds, he was transferred from the gun platform of his sinking ship to a lifeboat and then quickly conveyed to Tobruk hospital, where he died at midnight on 11 April. He was buried at Tobruk War Cemetery (grave no. 64), and was posthumously awarded the George Medal for devotion to duty.

Peggy Ball

Peggy Ball, who was Chairman of Seaton Town Council 1991–1993, was a Captain in the ATS in the Second World War. This is her story:

> I was 'called up' in August 1939, having joined the then ATS earlier in the year. 'You are going overseas', they said, but in fact we went to a Gunsight on the Isle of Wight, where I answered the telephone and helped in the office—in fact the five of us there were just general dogsbodies. Then early in 1940 I moved to an Operations room on the South Coast and became part of the Royal Signals. I spent most of the War at Uxbridge in the Operations room there, in charge of the Army Section. I then became an Instructor at Signals Training Schools at Kingston and St Neots, in between being in charge of a Signals Unit in South Wales before and after D-Day.

Peggy Ball, who was Chairman of Seaton Town Council 1991–1993, was a captain in the ATS during the Second World War. She is seen here in 1941.

I was demobilised in November 1945. Probably the most harrowing time was spent in the Operations room on the South Coast, with continuous air raids, at one time night and day.

SALUTE THE SISTER

We stood with hats off and thought about Sister Mac. We had not seen her for a couple of months but the days she took care of us in Ward 4D East in the British General Hospital in Naples seemed very close this afternoon.

A pale slender girl with dark hair and eyes, she was very conscious of the two pips upon her shoulder. The British call their nurses 'sister' but it is not a term of familiarity.

Miss Mac liked discipline and order. That was why she had such a hard time with Ward 4 where American field service volunteer ambulance drivers stayed when they were sick. We were unruly, untidy and sometimes a little impolite, which she could not understand at all. Some of us were there long enough to get to know her pretty well.

On Christmas Eve, I remember, somebody got hold of a bottle of brandy. We made milk punch in a hospital bucket and lured her in for a party. One of the boys had received a Christmas stocking from home, and on Christmas Day we turned it into a present for Sister Mac. We put in some cigarettes, candy and a cake of toilet soap and a little jar of cleansing cream which somebody had been carrying around. Wally put in one of his cigars and we filled up the rest with oranges and nuts.

Jack Green, 1943. Jack was born in 1923 and joined the Royal Navy at the outbreak of war, aged only sixteen. In 1942 he served on the Arctic convoys, taking supplies to Russia, around the North Cape and through Arctic Waters to Murmansk. These convoys were attacked by marauding aircraft and U-boats and their crews suffered incredible hardships, including frostbite. Jack was invalided out of the Navy because of his experiences, but he never regained full health, and died at the age of forty-seven. Jack could be described as one of Seaton's real heroes.

That day when she opened her drawer there it was, bulging and red, with a card saying 'Merry Christmas Miss Mac'. She picked it up and turned slowly to face us, the blood rushing to the roots of her hair. She opened her mouth just once but nothing came out, and then she ran from the room. But when she came back her hand was especially gentle as she took our pulses and tucked us in the sheets.

That was about three months ago.

The day before yesterday the Germans raided Naples and bombs fell on the hospital. So this afternoon, those of us who could get there, stood with our hats off and thought about Miss Mac. The coffin was incredibly small as it was lowered into the ground. And the tears rolled down our cheeks.

LAC R. W. Bennett 1240701

Reg Bennett was a Colyton man and a carpenter by trade. He and his wife, Winsome, had a house at Lees Farm, Southleigh, on her father's farm. After his medical in Exeter in November 1940, he was sent to Blackpool for training then to RAF Cosford for further training as a flight mechanic. He was posted to RAF Cranwell where he spent most of his war.

He kept a detailed diary of his whole war service which was, in the main routine, but there was some excitement. He played quite a bit of football, going with the team to play other units. He found digs, and Winsome was able to join him near Cranwell, and they often went to the pictures. The journey from Cranwell to Devon was difficult, involving changing trains several times, often overnight, but Reg was always keen to make the journey, to visit family and friends in Southleigh and Colyton, even for just two days' leave.

Here are a few snippets from the diaries:

Sunday 20 July 1941

V for Victory day for Britain. Walked to the camp, went in church where hymn singing was to be broadcast, had practice until 4.30 when we were on the air (can you hear me, mother?) We sang seven hymns, it was some of the good old hymns, we enjoyed it, there was about 6 to 800 people there.

The skill and endurance of the British tank crews in the Second World War are well documented. Originally a British invention and first used in the First World War, tanks played an important role during the Second World War and proved to be a match for the German Panzer Division. Ken Gould, photographed cleaning his equipment in Holland in 1944, was born in Dalwood in 1924. He joined the Army in 1942, serving in the Tank Corps as a mechanic and driver. Ken landed with his tank in Normandy on D-Day plus two, and was engaged in action throughout France, Belgium and Holland, finishing up in Germany, which he took part in the victory parade in Berlin.

Wednesday 4 August 1941

When we were marching back we saw a fire engine go onto the landing ground and wondered what was up. We found that one of the trainee pilots, who was on his first solo flight, had lost his nerve and was afraid to land. Then the ambulance arrived and the pilot came down to land, then took off again, he did this three or four times but he made up his mind at last and made a good landing. He then took his plane back to take off again, but after he had done quite a good run he gave up, and did not go up.

Friday 22 August 1941

Went to the camp to the pictures in the evening. Saw the News Reel of

Winston Churchill meeting President Roosevelt on board the *Prince of Wales*. They met last week for a few days.

Friday 26 September 1941

Another chap and myself went on at 10, had been out there for about an hour, when one of the planes about to land seemed to be coming down too steep and it was, it crashed, but no-one was hurt. The chap I was with went out to meet a plane that wanted to come in, and with the use of torches signalled him in, and in turning him round the plane crashed into another, so that was three planes useless.

Thursday 20 November 1941

Mock invasion. A sergeant took us over to the college where the enemy was, over we went but could not see anybody, then someone saw them go up behind one of the buildings, so we rushed up and were supposed to have captured them, and they said they captured us, so we don't know which were prisoners and don't think it matters much (sooner play Red Indians).

Petty Officer Bob 'Taffy' Pugsley, c. 1944. Taffy joined the Royal Navy in 1939 and served on HM Destroyer *Watchman* from 1940 to 1945, seeing service in the Mediterranean and Atlantic, and on the East Coast convoys. He was also involved in the Battle of the Atlantic from the beginning to the end. From 1945 until he left the Navy, Taffy was a PT instructor at HMS *Ariel* Training Camp. He came to East Devon in 1962 as entertainments manager at Warner's holiday camp in Seaton and became popular with the thousands of campers until his retirement in 1982.

Friday 20 March 1942

There was a nasty accident last Thursday night, one of the Whittley bombers which were doing night flying crashed into the college, which caused quite a large fire, but under control with the help of fire brigades from Sleaford, Lincoln, Newark and Grantham. There were three in the kite which were dead, and some casualties in the College, but none fatal.

Saturday 20 March 1943

Had bad news through on the 'phone, that two instructors, F/O Wheeler and F/Sgt Clarke, and also two pupils were killed in 477. It crashed into a balloon cable near Crewe, which was very sad.

Wednesday 8 September 1943

Heard that it had been broadcast from Algiers at 5.30 that Italy had made an Armistice with the Allies. Unconditional surrender, it was signed on 3 September.

Thursday 25 November 1943

Had a nasty accident at our Flight, an Oxford 458 which used to belong to us crashed, its undercarriage caught the roof of our offices, and crashed into a hut next to the crew hut and shook me rigid. We rushed out and tried to get the pilot out, but the flames got too fierce. It was a pupil in the kite, very sad.

Monday 17 April 1944

Had a new wireless op. and the first kite she got in, she fell off and broke her ankle. They fetched her in the ambulance.

Tuesday 6 June 1944

The 2nd Front, invasion of Normandy, France, took place between 6 and quarter to eight this morning. Had to stop night flying here to let the kites go over. There were 4,000 large ships and several thousand smaller ones used. They also had 11,000 planes ready for use if they were wanted.

Captain E. A. Stentiford (centre) with two colleagues, having just passed out successfully at OCTU in 1943. He served with the RASC and carried out the majority of his active service in the Second World War in Italy. When training to become an officer, he said the most gruelling part of the course was learning to become a motorbike dispatch rider, as he had a number of painful spills in the wilds of Northumberland. His army years may often have been fraught with danger, but the daily uncertainty which prevailed made them the most exciting time of his life. His most dangerous moment came at Bari in the southeast of Italy, where he was lucky to escape with his life after a massive explosion. An American liberty ship carrying ammunition blew up in Bari harbour on 4 January 1944, killing more than 2,000 Allied soldiers and sailors and Italian civilians. Many victims were blown into the sea, and about 1,000 families were left homeless. A colleague who was with Captain Stentiford caught the full blast and was killed instantly, but mercifully Captain Stentiford, although injured and suffering deafness for some months, recovered to continue his duties. On his return home at the end of the war he worked at Lloyds Bank, Seaton, where he became assistant bank manager.

10,000 tons of bombs were dropped on invasion targets from midnight to 8 am, and 7,500 sorties flown.

Thursday 3 August 1944

The King returned to England after a twelve-day tour of the battle fronts in Italy. Turkey broke relations with Germany.

Friday 2 February 1945

Had to go on guard duty. We challenged a bloke, who after a time answered but did not say much, so we let him go then doubled back around the drome, and challenged him again. We still could not get much out of him, so let him go again for a while and as he was hanging around the drome, we were getting cheesed off with him, so had a good go at him. First he wanted us to shoot him, then he wanted to borrow the rifle to shoot himself, it appeared a girl had let him down, and he seemed in a bad way. We eventually got him to move up into the camp, and went off guard at 8.

Friday 15 March 1946

By tube to Uxbridge for release, had to wait in the Naaffi until our names were called then got paid etc. From Uxbridge we went to Wembley to choose our clothes, and some job it was, not much choice.

Tom Newton of Seaton at Buckingham Palace with his wife Rene after receiving the BEM. Having served with distinction in the First World War, Tom joined the Home Guard in the Second World War. He was awarded the BEM for securing and rendering safe a mine in the River Axe.

Ex-Petty Officer Motor Mechanic
G. Swales, Engineer on HM LCT 1137

During the course of landing American troops on Omaha Beach, our landing craft sustained substantial damage to the bow area. After examining the damage it was decided that we should be able to make the return journey to our base in Portland, Dorset. However, after two or three hours at sea, the weather changed for the worse and the sea became very rough.

In the middle of the night, in mid Channel, due to a combination of being battered by the waves and the previously sustained damage, the landing craft broke in two. We were obliged to heave to and set to work securing the two sections of the craft together, using the chains which were supplied to us for use in securing tanks or other vehicles, to prevent them moving during transit. Working in pitch darkness this took several hours, but eventually we were able to get under way and resume our journey. Due to the damaged state of the landing craft it proved extremely difficult to navigate and the skipper decided to make for the first piece of land we saw,

Daphne Harman Young sitting on part of the landing craft wrecked on Seaton Beach, 1944.

which happened to be the seaside resort of Seaton in Devon.

The landing craft was beached between Seaton Hole and The Chine. The crew scrambled ashore and made their way through the sea defences of barbed wire and concrete 'tank trap' pyramids, up Fore Street to the Town Hall, where they found the Caretaker, who lived in upstairs flat. They stayed in Seaton for a week and were looked after by the Town Council and the WRVS, before being sent home on Survivors' Leave for a week.

The landing craft eventually broke in two and the half on which I am sitting drifted to opposite the Beach Hotel, now Whitecliffe Flats, on the East Walk. It remained there until the 1950s, much to the delight of local children, who had many happy hours playing on 'The Wreck', as it was known.

George Ambrose Swales
14 April 1925-28 January 2008

The British Legion National Standard Bearer was present at his funeral in Durham, 7 February 2008.

My Story—A Colyford Man

War broke out on 3 September 1939 and I got my calling up papers on the 16 October 1939. I had to travel to Exeter, joining the Devonshire Regt. and I arrived with a couple of dozen other chaps. Having been issued with our kit, we had a regulation haircut, and the dreaded needle stuck in.

Next morning we got up to the sound of the bugle, breakfast, then it was time for our first parade. We were lined up in threes on the square, and orders were shouted out by the sergeant. We would have liked to tell the sergeant that we did have parents, but thought better of it. After about six weeks we began to look like soldiers, by this time we knew who to salute and who not to.

A short time after that I was taken ill and I was transferred by ambulance to Plymouth Naval Hospital for four weeks, then I was taken to Westbury in Wiltshire for convalescence for about six weeks.

Back in army routine, I spent a few more weeks at Exeter before joining the Queens RR at Caterham. A few days later we were on our way to France, where they made us a working battalion, so we were away from the Germans for a while. After two weeks we were moved forward nearer the enemy, I could now hear the guns. The Germans were pushing the British army thick and fast, so we didn't stay there long, we started the long march

Gerald Abbot, here in 1940, was born in Grapevine Terrace, Branscombe and was known to his many friends as 'Ger'. He was called up in 1939 and served abroad with the 4th Battalion Devonshire Regiment. He died in 1991.

back towards the coast. We were marching every night and resting during the day, by now a lot of the chaps looked very rough.

One of the days, our section of five men were told to go out and see where the Germans were, we didn't get close enough find them, but we did get mixed up with the refugees that were swarming the roads. We decided to get clear of them, as Jerry often came and machine-gunned them, so we made our way across the fields away from the roads. We had lost the battalion, so we were on our own. I can't remember how long we were walking before we came to the coast, but it cheered us up, until we saw thousands of other chaps there. The place was called St Vallery, it didn't seem as though we had much of a chance of getting away, but we got down to the beach and there we sat all night long. The following morning we saw a few ships on the horizon, we hoped they would get to us before Jerry did. As daylight approached, the ships came nearer, but they could not get close enough to pick us up.

This is where our training came in. We all lined up down to the waterfront, hoping that the Jerries would not come over and machine gun us. Luck was on our side, small boats came up to the beach, and after a

Peggy Ball, a captain in the ATS, seen in St Neots in 1945, is second from the left in the front row. She was later Chairman of Seaton Town Council.

long time we were picked up and taken out to the big boats.

The next we knew we were sailing into Dover, we went on deck and saw the White Cliffs, a lot of us had tears in our eyes. We arrived at Devizes about two o'clock in the morning, and stayed there for a few days rest, then the five of us were sent back to our company. We had to travel up to Newcastle to a place called Haltwhistle, and we were sent home the next day on a two-day leave.

We were moved around to quite a few places. The last one we were at was called Long Melford. When we got called out to be measured for our tropical kit, we guessed where we were going next—we looked quite smart in our shorts and topee. We were soon on the train on our way to Liverpool. When we saw the ship, bigger than a four-storey building, we thought, 'if we got bombed in that it would be impossible for him to miss'.

After about three weeks at sea we arrived at Cape Town, a beautiful place, where we managed to get ashore for a couple of days sightseeing, it seemed strange to see everywhere lit up with no blackout. Our next stop was Bombay, we were there for three weeks. We then left India, on a rather old tramp steamer, which soon took us to Baghdad, we were under canvas there, guarding ammunition dumps. By now it must be 1942 or 1943, we were in Iraq for quite a few months, nothing very exciting happened.

We then left there by road, we found out we were going into action in the desert. It took us a month by road, passing through a number of countries. We caught some of the fighting, but the desert war finished soon after—we were quite lucky, but we did lose a few men.

The unit was then stationed in Tripoli, training for the invasion of Italy. It was on the eighth of September that we boarded the landing barges, and we were sailing through the night. The next day we heard over the tannoy that the Italians had packed it in, there was a great cheer as we all thought we would just go to Italy to police it, but it didn't work out that way. Jerry was waiting for us.

We arrived at Salerno early in the morning, but the boats couldn't go right into the shore, so we had to jump off into the sea. We had to get off the beach as quickly as possible, as there were troops coming ashore from other boats. I'm afraid my mate Bert was killed. He must have stepped on a mine. Our first object was to capture an airfield, we were on one side of the field and the Germans were on the other side. Our Officer was killed here, shame, he was a very nice bloke. One of our Bren gun carriers got hit by shellfire and the bodies of the men were burning. It was a horrible smell. Just after that one of our spitfires tried to land, not realising that Jerry still had the field in his hands, no sooner had he landed they caught him and he went up in flames.

When we went up to the front we took up positions just in front of the Germans—they might be about three or four hundred yards in front of you. They would be dug in, we would take up position and dig in, usually done by night. Two of you dug a trench about four foot deep, so you had a fair bit of cover, and we might be up there for about three to four days. After about four days we were relieved by another company then we went out of the line for a rest, that was about three miles back. By this time we were losing quiet a good few of our chaps, either killed or wounded.

During the time I was out of the line we did get a pass to go to Naples and who should I bump into but my brother Albert – I didn't even know he was in Italy. After the rest period we went back in the line, we were getting quite close to Casino by now, but we missed that and were sent to Anzio, which was very rough. The weather was terrible, we were walking ankle deep in mud. After leaving Anzio with no regrets, we left Italy and went

Harry Good from Seaton in his RAF uniform.

over to a little island off Yugoslavia, we were there for about a month.

After that back to Italy and we went straight into action. I think it was called the Gothic Line? This is where I got wounded and where I was taken by plane to a Naples hospital, and Albert came to visit me. I was in there for a few weeks, then to the convalescent camp. The doctors said I could not go back into the Infantry, and I got a job with the Regimental Police in the transport company, life was much easier. By this time the war was over, and I was on my way home for a whole month of leave.

We crossed the channel, and I got home to find a big banner across the house saying, 'Welcome Home George', I felt quite proud.

I had a good time in fact I think it was my best time in the Army. I was sorry when my demob came through, I was sorry that I had to leave them.

My story ends here. I was one of the lucky ones who was able to write a story like this.

1931–1945 LOCAL HERO

This account took place on a December morning in 1940. Tom Newton, a local fisherman and a member of the Home Guard, left his Harbour Cottage to find himself staring at a German mine bobbing along the River Axe on the incoming tide. It was heading upstream on a possible collision course with Axmouth Bridge, packed with enough explosive to blow the side off a battleship. Fortunately several fathoms of cable attached to the mine were slowing its progress, but it was drifting dangerously close to the harbour wall.

Tom fetched an oar from his cottage, and used it to prod the mine away. Glancing over his shoulder, he noticed his wife and a friend looking curiously at what he was doing. He politely told them that he thought they would be better off indoors, considering the circumstances. For over two hours Tom manoeuvred the mine, keeping it away from the harbour wall, but still it dragged its cable ominously towards the bridge. There was, however, some comfort in the knowledge that the tide was about to turn.

A hazardous situation was made worse by the fact that there were two trainloads of naval ammunition standing at Seaton railway station, just beyond the bridge. During the war Beer Quarry was an underground ammunition dump for the Royal Navy, and these two train loads were standing in the siding, waiting to be unloaded and then transported by road to the Quarry.

Eventually the tide turned and Tom warily escorted the mine back towards the sea, still gingerly warding it away from the wall with his oar to avoid any chance of a sharp tap on its detonating horns. At the mouth of the river he waded into the water and coaxed the mine onto a spit of shingle, where the receding tide left it high and dry. The Axmouth Coastguard were called to dehorn and neutralise it, and the danger was over.

A grateful town held a whip-round for him, and the Admiralty gave him £5—a generous amount for those days, but worth every penny for the deed he performed. King George VI awarded Tom Newton the Order of the British Empire for his bravery. Pinning the medal on Tom's Home Guard tunic at the Buckingham Palace Investiture, the King remarked 'It was an extremely plucky thing to do, and I congratulate you on your escape'.

Tom Newton died in 1971. During his last years he sold fish from a small blue Austin van at Fisherman's Gap on Seaton sea front.

Those Who Served

Eileen (Lan) Mutter of Seaton in her VAD nursing uniform. Back in 1942 when Eileen joined, the Seaton detachment met at the TOC.H rooms, which were in Queen Street along the little alleyway that also served as the back door to the George Inn.

Harry Small

Harry Small from Sidmouth was killed in Italy during the last months of the Second World War. He was my uncle, and this letter to my Aunt Edith was from his Commanding Officer:

Dear Mrs Small,

Thank you for your letter and again I must say how much I sympathise with you.

I have made enquiries for someone name of Paddy who was a friend of Harry. It was a man who was posted from the Company some time ago. However, I am putting the address at the end of the letter in case you care to write to him.

I have also asked for Harry's particular friend and I am told it was Taffy Jones. I have seen this man and he says he will be writing to you.

When Harry was hit he lost consciousness and died soon afterwards, so that he was unable to give any last messages. But a .... was in attendance.

No doubt you will have received, or will soon receive, some money which was collected by the men of this Company. It was a purely voluntary act, and I think every man contributed towards the £55 which has been forwarded to you.

Please accept this as a gift from my Company, expressing their sympathy to you and in memory of a brave good man.

Sincerely, Kenneth Hollingsworth, Major.
Commanding 848 Smoke Coy. PC.

Flight Sergeant Bill Smith

We have a great deal of modern criticism about the bombing of Hitler's cities. I hold no brief with this. I remember well the destruction of Exeter and Plymouth, and many other English cities. The Lancaster was the British bomber used, and of the 7,377 Lancasters built, 3,932 were lost in action.

Flight Sergeant W. (Bill) Smith, only son of Edgar Smith of Seaton, was

Harry Small from Sidmouth, who was killed in Italy during the last months of the Second World War.

reported missing on 13 February 1944 when he took part in a Lancaster raid on Berlin. He was never found. Two days before he was killed, he wrote the following letter to his best friend, Seaton boy Douglas Littley, nickname Nib:

Dear Nib,

Just a line to let you know how things are going once again. Thanks for the mail. I received one of your letters OK on return from leave and the other last week. Talking of leave reminds me, we are due for our second fourteen days in about a fortnight's time.

Well Nib, things have been on the top line recently. Our pilot received an immediate award of the DFC for fourteen trips to Berlin – see the citation in the papers this week. Our vradio op also had the DFC, so things are looking up.

On top of that, we were introduced to the King and Queen last

Three Seaton boys pose for this photograph, taken on the West Cliff about 1937. Left to right, Boyce Anning, who was to die under tragic circumstances during the post-war years, Bill Smith, who joined Bomber Command and was killed on 13 February 1944, and Douglas Littley (Nib).

Thursday. I spoke to both of them and shook hands with the Queen. Gee – but she is marvellous.

Yes, the general idea is for us to pack up for good after the next fifteen trips. If I get through OK I shall have seen enough excitement for one war.

Let me know if you come up this way and I will see what can be fixed up.

By the way I wish they would put the Home Guard on the German Flak Guns.

Guess that's about all till next time, so over to you.

Cheers, all the best from Bill

When I read this letter and write about the other young Seaton and Beer boys who lost their lives, tears prick my eyes and I become haunted by the reflection of what did medals mean to them, compared to the travesty of extinction?

5

Nestlecombe and Branscombe
The War Years

On the outbreak of war, new factories for the munitions drive were soon planned. Sydney Pritchard and his brother William won a contract to produce shell fuses and aircraft components. Their factory in Holloway, North London, was moved to the garage in Branscombe Square. This is their story.

> Anyone visiting the attractive Square today would find it difficult to realise what a hive of industry took place there during the war. It all happened like this ...
> A company by the name of Nestlé (no, not the chocolate firm), C. Nestle & Company, of which a Mr Nestler was the originator, very many years ago invented a treatment for ladies' hair, to provide a permanent wave. As we all know, this became, and still is, very popular. In pre-war days it involved the use of heat as well as chemicals, and to provide this heat machines were made, and of course hairdryers and other hairdressing requirements. Nestle designed, patented and produced this special top quality electrical equipment and had their Head Office and Factory in Holloway, North London.
> With the commencement of hostilities not unnaturally the demand for this equipment ceased, and the company was invited by the Ministry of Supply to undertake war work, its machinery and other plant being ideally suitable for the purpose in mind. It soon became apparent that the workshops were no longer big enough, nor ideal, and an approach to the Ministry advised us that they would be willing to move the plant and the key personnel, but we had first to find suitable premises and go back to them with a proposition.
> Armed with a liberal supply of petrol coupons we set forth to the Torbay area, having had many happy holidays in the district we knew that part of the country possibly better than any other. It was when we were working our way back that we contacted a large garage in Sidmouth

Interior view of Nestlés Munitions Factory, Branscombe, c. 1943. On the outbreak of war new factories for the munitions drive were soon planned and Sydney Pritchard and his brother William won a contract to produce shell fuses and aircraft components. Their factory in Holloway, North London, was moved to the garage in Branscombe Square.

and explained our requirements. The Proprietor said he knew of just the place and would be pleased to escort us to the building. This turned out to be a brand new garage in Branscombe, of no less than 6,000 square feet floor area, with a flat and showroom facing The Square. It had been built for a Mr Dowell, who operated the Orange & Black Bus Company, which ran a local service from Seaton to Sidmouth and had built his new headquarters to be halfway, so to speak, between the two towns. However, with the coming of the war he decided to sell up and the building therefore was available to purchase. All it needed to turn it into a factory was to install a heating system, build various outhouses for supplies to be stored and a canteen on the little piece of land that was left between the end of the factory and the Police Station.

The Ministry were delighted with our acquisition and the move was agreed, with a dozen or so more key personnel. To arrange accommodation for these people was another problem, but the Beach House Hotel in Beer had closed and the company were able to run it fully furnished for

On 14 November 1940 Ernest Bevin, Minister of Labour and National Service, said that women were needed and would be trained side by side with men in skilled work as munitions workers. The ladies pictured here in 1943 worked in the secret wartime factory at Branscombe which produced millions of shell fuses and aircraft components.

a period of one year as a staff hostel. This proved very satisfactory and within the year everyone had made their own arrangements.

As engineers we specialised in the production of what is known as turn parts and made numerous items for the aeroplane and other industries, but the main contract which ran throughout the war was for the production of Orlecon shell fuses, a three part component which was completed in a matter of six seconds. Millions of these fuses were produced for the Navy's use.

Such production did of course upset normal village life to some extent. Fifteen-ton lorry loads of brass bar used to arrive every week, such loads breaking many manhole covers and cutting off hedges, to say nothing of the loads leaving the Factory. What was even more amazing was that we worked round the clock, two twelve hour shifts, eight to eight, but closing at midday on Saturday and re-commencing at the 8 o'clock shift on Sunday evening. During the intermediary time, maintenance staff moved in to service the machinery.

Government regulations insisted that all factories, on the pretence of keeping staff happy, had to have music while you work – a bigger misnomer would be impossible to find. The machinery made such a noise that the loudspeakers had to be at full blast to overcome that noise – and in the middle of the night. Although we never thought of it much at the time, we have since wondered why we were never bombed, since we feel sure that the noise could have been heard even in a small aeroplane, and there was no defence between Branscombe beach and The Square—and for that matter we did not even have air-raid shelters nor was there one anywhere in the village.

There were of course lighter moments. The main production being a Naval requirement meant that we had to have a Navy inspection within the factory, and a Lieutenant Commander made the Inspection once a week, usually arriving in time for lunch, in a Bentley driven by a Wren. We were immediately summoned to join him at the Masons almost opposite, in those days a small hostelry consisting of one small bar and the dining room, which had one large table in the centre on which the pickled onions and cheese and bread were served. The Masons in those days was run by one Charlie Clark a confirmed not so young bachelor, but we ended all that—he married one of our ladies that we brought with us from London.

Another memorable occasion was the year we had a snowstorm the likes of which have never been seen since. The snow was so heavy it settled on telephone and electric wires and then froze, with the result that the weight was more than the wires could stand and they came down all over the place. Roads were more or less impassable, but Mr Oborn, who ran the garage in Beer which operated a couple of taxis, managed to keep going and run as far as the top of Branscombe Hill, then staff and others had to walk the rest.

In the village square there were three shops, and their supplies were beginning to run short. The shell fuses were dispatched in special wooden boxes, and to overcome the shops' supply situation, we made a train of these boxes, tying a dozen or more together and then tugged them up the hill to the waiting taxi which had the goods to deliver— and then slid them down as a long sleigh, and so the shops were replenished. In spite of the snow and all the hazards it brought with it, we managed to keep going the whole time.

In those days the Nestle factory employed some 120 full or part-time staff, almost everybody in the village and surrounding district had worked for us at some time or another. Many of us also did Home Guard and Warden duties and were therefore fully alive to the impending D-

On 14 November 1940 Ernest Bevin, Minister of Labour and National Service, said that women were needed and would be trained side-by-side with men in skilled work as munition workers. The ladies pictured here in 1943 worked in the secret wartime factory at Branscombe which produced millions of shell fuses and aircraft components.

Day preparations, but apart from the fact that there was a little more tension building up, everybody proceeded fairly as normal.

Locally there was evidence of preparations, for example in the Beer Road, Seaton, there was a camp of Nissen huts on land starting where the Old Beer Road joins New, on which many bungalows have since been built. This camp was occupied by contingents from many countries who made themselves popular, and the Americans were the last and left just before D-Day. There was also a Nissen hut on the flat part of the ground in the Chine. Indeed the floor and foundations are still there but covered up with soil. This was used by the Home Guard, who spent many a night sleeping an hour or two on the floor.

In addition the holiday camp in Seaton, apart from being an internment camp to start with, also later became the home of various troops waiting for D-Day.

You may wonder what happened to it all. Well, Nestle continued to use it after peace was declared for a year or two to try and become re-established in its legitimate trade. Things had altered however, so much so that hair waving did not require the heat and therefore the machines,

Ted Manville, who came down from London when the Nestlecombe Factory moved to Branscombe in 1940, is pictured here after the war, working at Shands in Axminster.

other than driers. It was therefore decided to wind up the Company and, for the record, the Name, Patents and Trademarks were purchased by the other Nestlé Company.

The premises continued with the manufacture of some electronic equipment for a time, then again as a garage, but ultimately a developer came along. They demolished the factory/garage building and built some houses on the site which incidentally, contained a lovely orchard which produced very sweet apples. The office block or flat which boasted of having one of the only six baths in Branscombe, is still there and restored to its legitimate purpose—Nestlecombe House.

Out of the ashes, PECO was started in a two-room cottage next to Colliers shop, but that is another story.

6

Sidmouth

Much excitement and anticipation was felt by the people in Sidmouth as local men were serving in the Navy, the Army, the Air Force and the Reserves. The air raid precautions committee was also busy. In Sidmouth, more than 500 air-raid alerts were sounded and the town was occasionally machine-gunned from the air, with enemy pilots disposing of some bombs which had been intended for Exeter. The sea front was barricaded with barbed wire and scaffolding with some entrances to the beach blocked with concrete 'tank trap' pyramids. There was access to the sea front from the market and Clifton slipway, where a life-like imitation cottage housed a gun. A coastal-defence battery was established in the Connaught Gardens and Army and RAF contingents were stationed in the town. The grounds of The Knowle were used as a training area for commandos.

On 1 September 1939, two days before war was declared, the first evacuation scheme from London and other big cities began to operate and, within a few days, the first contingent arrived. By October 1940, Sidmouth had accepted almost 4,000 evacuees. The Sidmouth members of the voluntary organisations achieved wonders in finding accommodation for them all.

By the end of 1940 strict food rationing was introduced and people were encouraged to 'dig for victory' by growing their own food in their gardens and allotments. Blackout material was in great demand to cover the windows at night and strict control was exercised on householders by the ARP and special constabulary. Special 'war savings weeks' were held at intervals between 1941 and 1945, these comprising War Weapons Week, Warship Week, Wings for Victory Week, Salute the Soldier Week and Thanksgiving Week.

As D-Day approached, the area of East Devon became very active as American troops were dispersed in the lanes and woods. When the great

Seaton and East Devon in the Second World War

Sidmouth

day came, all the troops suddenly disappeared overnight. At long last, on 8 May 1945, peace was declared in Europe and a two-day holiday was given to all. Free entertainment, communal lunches and tea parties were held in the streets of Sidmouth.

The Sidmouth Observer Corps rendered valuable service during the Second World War. There were observer posts over the entire country, where a day and night watch was kept for the sight or sound of enemy aircraft. Britain's defences were set in motion by these lonely and devoted watchers in their far-flung outposts as they plotted the course of any enemy raiders. The Sidmouth observer post opened in 1943 on the top of Peak Hill and was numbered 21 Group Exeter, Post E3. Manned by local volunteers on a part-time basis, it was a concrete structure with a downstairs room and a walled upper storey where observations of aircraft were carried out. There was also a satellite post on Salcombe Hill which was connected by telephone to the Peak Hill post.

In November 1953 the Sidmouth post was re-numbered Post W4 of 10 Group Exeter. During July 1962 the above-ground post was demolished and an underground post constructed, complete with instruments for monitoring nuclear radiation—it was changed to 52 post of 9 Group Yeovil. In 1991, after nearly fifty years of devoted service, the Corps stood down and the underground post was filled in.

By the end of the war, the spirit of the nation had changed; no one in 1945 wanted to go back to 1939. With the slogan, 'victory at all costs', the British people had won and were now fully confident to go forward to the future. Party politics returned to centre stage and a general election took place on 5 July which swept Labour back into power, headed by Clement

Opposite above: Sector 109 Fireguards, Exmouth, 1944. Fireguards played their part in civilian defence during the Second World War. During air raids they patrolled various areas on the lookout for incendiary bombs. Front row, left to right: G. Howe-Haysome, W. Hall, A. Dommett, J. Southwell, H. Hynard, W. Bond, G. Hall, B. H. Avery (sector captain), P. Milford, R. Ridley, A Carpenter, L. Bradford, A. Moist, ? Moist, H. A. Johnson. Second row: D. Dymond, E. Madge, E. Letten, E. Smith, I. Tozer, L. Stubbington, M. Fryer, A. Roach, L. Underwood, A. Thompson, V. Dobel. Third Row: M. Tucker, D. Seagroatt, E. Richards, E. Pidgeon, D. Salmon, L. Bell, E. Williams, M. Oxford, K. Maers, D. Southwell, M. Ridley, F. Humphries. Back row, left to right: H. Bond, A. Backhouse, M. Bond.

Opposite below: Exmouth experienced its own Blitz on 18 January 1941, when an indiscriminate bombing raid was made on the town. This is Chapel Street the morning after the raid, with members of the AFS and ARP examining the rubble.

Seaton and East Devon in the Second World War

Attlee as Premier. The Conservatives had relied on the glory of Churchill's name, but the Labour Party offered a programme for the future. Even so, East Devon, with Sidmouth, remained true blue and Cedric Drewe kept this seat for the Conservatives.

Opposite above: Sidmouth Observer Corps 1944. Left to right, back row: Messrs Martin, Lindo, Lake, Perry, Woolley, Pearce, Ashby, Johns, Spurway. Front row, seated: Messrs Thorn, Lowe, Miss O'Hara, Messrs Mills, Mills, Eveleigh, Newton, King, Beacon.

Opposite below: Firemen searching the wreckage of Walton's Store, Exmouth 1941.

7
Small Talk from Seaton
Ted Gosling and Gerald Gosling Remember

I was ten years old when Great Britain declared war on Germany in 1939. What did it mean, that we were at war? I had no idea what it meant, except that some terrible event was about to happen, but I remember well that Sunday morning in September 1939 when, walking up Homer Lane with friends, we were stopped by Seaton man Tom Pavey and told we were at war.

One of the first things my father did was to dig an air-raid shelter in our back garden, it soon flooded and we never used it.

One of my earliest recollections was the National Day of Prayer. In what is still called the 'miracle of Dunkirk' 300,000 British troops were rescued from the beaches of France in an operation fraught with danger. King George VI requested that Sunday 26 May 1940 should be observed as a National Day of Prayer, to help our troops. Millions of people all over the country flocked to the churches, and Seaton Parish Church was so full that people stood outside.

Three miracles followed:

1) Hitler over-ruled his generals and halted the advance of his armoured columns
2) A storm of unprecedented fury broke out, and the darkness of the storm meant that there was scarcely any interruption from aircraft
3) Despite the storm a great calm such as has rarely been experienced settled over the English Channel during the evacuation.

A coincidence, or power of prayer, I leave that for you to decide, dear reader. Even today we still use the expression, 'the Dunkirk spirit' to describe the ability of the British people to pull together.

In 1940 I was a pupil at Sir Walter Trevelyan School, still the Sir Walter Trevelyan Building, but now the Axe Valley Children's Centre, and I was

Small Talk from Seaton Ted Gosling and Gerald Gosling Remember

Seaton Scout Band pose for this photograph in Cross Street, Seaton, c. 1943.

selected to be an enemy plane observer when the air raid siren sounded. I used to patrol the rear playground and, being good at aircraft recognition, if I spotted an enemy aircraft I would rush into the classroom and warn everybody.

Late in 1940 my father was called up to serve in the Devonshire Regiment, based in Exeter. I used to help him look after two allotments, and at the age of twelve I took them over when he joined up. At that time allotments were helping to feed the nation, and by 1943 1.5 million plots were being cultivated. I grew potatoes and carrots, with a few cabbage plants.

Grandfather Gosling, who lived next door to where I live today, in Harepath Road, kept bees and was allowed a special sugar ration to help him keep the bees alive during the winter. This was to help not only to produce honey, but also to pollinate the fruit trees. During 1942 I used to work weekends in Andy Bartlett's Nursery gardens, with his large greenhouses full of tomato plants.

Compared with what we consume today, the level of provision under rationing does seem very small. My mother was allowed less than a pound

Seaton Scout Band on parade in Cross Street, Seaton, c. 1943. The band was playing for the opening ceremony of the Seaton, Colyton, Beer and District Wings for Victory Week on Saturday, 22 May 1943. The target for the week was £50,000, which would have bought one bomber and two Typhoons. Members of the band included Ron Anning, Bill Green, Ted Gosling, Ray Turner Bill Moulding, Don Rodgers and Ray Fox. Standing to the left of the band is the Scoutmaster, 'Skipper' Brookes.

of meat per person a week, and only two ounces of cheese. One good thing was that from the summer of 1940 all school children were given free milk, delivered to my school in two big churns. By 1943 milk consumption had risen by thirty per cent, potatoes by more than forty per cent, and the good news was that consumption of sugar was down by a third. We certainly enjoyed a more balanced and healthy diet than the children today. People were even better fed, thanks to the efforts of British farmers.

When scoutmaster 'Skipper' Brookes reformed the Seaton Scouts in 1941, I joined with many of my school friends, and became a member of the scout band, playing the bass drum. We used to have weekly band practice in the Vicarage field—now Case Gardens. The Seaton scout band played for many wartime events, including the 'Warship Week' and the 'Wings for Victory' week.

W. L. Oborn's garage in wartime Beer, 1943.

Scouts were also invited to be messenger boys with the ARP. I joined up with Len Northcott, and we were issued with a black ARP overcoat and a beret marked ARP. In the event of an air raid we would be on duty to carry messages if normal communications were down. Although we took turns to be on duty during a night-time warning, we were never required. I must confess that I found the idea of cycling through a bomb-damaged Seaton with fires everywhere did have a certain appeal to a thirteen-year old.

I left school in April 1943 at the age of fourteen to work as an apprentice motor mechanic in Oborn's Townsend Garage, Beer. All private cars were laid up and the only vehicles on the road at the time were used for essential work. In those wartime years it was a case of make do and mend to keep vehicles on essential work on the road. Tyres, timing chains and other spares were impossible to get. Pool petrol played havoc with exhaust valves and when they burnt out they had to be built up with a welding process called Bright Ray. On my way to work I used to pass the Nissen huts occupied by the Americans at the corner where Old Beer Road meets New Beer Road. Early in the morning you could smell the coffee brewing, and they always gave me a cheery wave.

Those wartime years spent working in the village of Beer were, for me, happy times. The folk of Beer then, as now, were warm-hearted people and strangers were always made welcome. Mr Oborn belonged to the Beer Home Guard and, following a night on duty, many of his fellow Home Guard members, such as Ted Mutter, would drop into the garage and would discuss the previous night's duties, and I would listen enthralled.

At Beer the stone quarries were used by the Admiralty as an ammunition store and day after day lorries full of ammunition would leave Seaton station and pass the garage on the way to the quarries. This was reversed in May 1944, when the lorries came down full and returned empty. We guessed that something would be happening and, of course, Operation Sea Lord took place on 6 June and we realised then where the ammunition was wanted.

The Bomb Disposal Units of the Royal Engineers had the thankless task of digging out and making safe the many unexploded bombs that fell on England during the Second World War. Pictured here during May 1944, the men of one such unit are working on the unexploded bomb in Paizen Lane, Beer.

In May 1944 an unexploded bomb fell in Paizen Lane, and a Bomb Disposal Unit of the Royal Engineers appeared, to have the task of digging it out and making it safe. It took about three weeks, and every morning they would walk down to the garage for a coffee and biscuit. I thought they were especially brave men, and hoped they survived the war.

When the war ended we were all given two days' holiday and I attended two celebrations, a wonderful night with dancing and a bonfire in Eyewell Green, and the Victory celebrations in Beer.

My brother, Gerald Gosling, who died in 2010, was a well-known author and a Colyton grammar school pupil. In this article he recalls his wartime Grammar School experiences:

> One of the first changes at the school saw a rash of crisscross muslin on every class room window, its purpose being to minimise the effect of glass splinters on pupils in the event of any bombs being dropped near the school. Also, the main hall and one classroom were fitted with blackout curtains to make sure that a room was always available for any school activity after dark.
>
> Almost immediately evacuees arrived in the Axe Valley, including the girls from the James Allen's School at Dulwich, many of whom came to Colyton Grammar School, helping to swell the pupil population to over 200. Mr McKay Ohm and his staff coped by using the hall balcony above the kitchen as a classroom, staggering lunch hours, packing as many children as possible into each classroom and sometimes using one of the laboratories as a make-shift classroom.
>
> The school became a centre for local fund raising including a series of whist drives in the hall, which brought in much-needed cash for the Spitfire Fund, and various items of 'comforts' were made or knitted and sent to the Red Cross Society. Troops stationed locally were allowed to use the sports field and the school's soccer 1st XI played—and usually beat—a team from the RAF's air-sea-rescue station at Lyme Regis.
>
> Pupils, if memories serve correctly, all boys, were taken by army lorry, usually to Stafford Common, where rough ground had been cultivated to grow potatoes in response to the Government's request to everyone to 'Dig For Victory'. The boys were paid for the work, and the odd ones were occasionally cuffed around the ear by an irate farmer for starting up their version of World War Three with hectic battles using the 'spuds' as ammunition.
>
> At least one boy from Seaton, but his name is not really important, was reported to the school for his potato-throwing exploits. And, not only was his name recorded in that infamous chronicle of school crime

known as the detention book, he later made a less-than-social call to the headmaster's study where the thing most people notice, when touching their toes in readiness for the application of the cane, are Grantland Rice's framed (and famed) words, 'When the one Great Scorer comes to mark against your name'.

More digging for victory arrived when the top half of the playing fields were turned into an allotment, thus helping both the war effort and the school's budget, most of the produce ending up in the kitchen.

Some older boys joined 'Dad's Army' and, on occasion, would arrive at school in the morning in uniform after spending the night straining their eyes for a glimpse of the Werhmacht heading for Colyton Grammar School. They would never have been allowed in, of course. Mr Mckay Ohm would have soon sent them packing for a whole number of reasons, starting with not being properly dressed in school uniform. With one-upmanship never before or since matched, one stalwart school member of the Home Guard brought his 303 Lee Enfield to school where he propped it up beside his desk.

This is 1067 ATC Squadron which was formed at Colyton Grammar School during the Second World War. The three officers in the front row, all members of the school staff, are Mr Jowett, Mr Montgomery and Mr Slade.

An ATC (Air Training Corp) squadron was formed at the school under Mr Jowett, and members wore their uniforms to school on the days when their twice-weekly meetings were held immediately after school ended for the day. Their squadron number was 1067, which led Mr Pointon, the history teacher, whose career at the school was interrupted by service in the Forces between 1941–45, to call them the Hastings-Plus-One brigade.

Rationing, including that of petrol, was always a problem, the latter causing Mr Weeks of Southleigh, a governor, to offer to resign because of the difficulty in travelling in from Southleigh. He was persuaded to continue after an attempt was made to get him an extra petrol ration. Even as late as 1947 the school's ration for an entire year was just 60 gallons.

The paper shortage led to the pupils being introduced into the habit of ignoring margins in their exercise books, but not for the Physics or Maths lessons held by Mr Bingham between 1941-45. 'Sarge', as he was universally known, was an arthritic, hard-of-hearing, irascible former teacher who had retired to Colyford and, despite being well into his seventies, offered his services for the duration. He was one of the old school and no German was going to make his pupils do without margins.

Thousands of American soldiers were billeted in the district during the lead-up to D-Day, including some in the field that then existed just below the boy's entrance and behind the junction of Elm Farm Lane and Gulley Shute. Needless to say, their generosity led to a plague of worn-out gum stuck under most desks, certainly in a certain third form of the time, and the smell of Camels and Lucky Strike cigarette smoke was said to have stayed in the boys' toilets well past the end of the hostilities in Europe which, when it arrived in 1945, saw the entire school gathered in the hall to give thanks to God, Mr Churchill and the Armed Forces. They then all departed to enjoy the two-day holiday kindly given to the nation by the said Mr Churchill.

8

The Final Victory

As the spring of 1945 progressed, every day brought more news of the Liberation of Europe until finally, the day of victory arrived. The instrument of unconditional surrender was signed on the 17 May 1945 to take effect on the following day. During the evening of 7 May, patrons of the Royal Cinema in Seaton stood up and cheered when the cinema lights went up at 9 p.m. and the cinema manager, Mr Crawford announced that war in Germany was over. This must have been the proudest and most emotional moment of his life.

At last, on 8 May 1945, peace in Europe came and a two-day holiday was declared. Although the seafront was still barricaded with barbed wire and concrete 'tank trap' pyramids, the threat of invasion was over and no more air-raid alerts were sounded. But everyone knew that further names had been added to the lists of those who had been killed in the First World War: a fact that must remind future generations of the terrible cost of war.

Free entertainment, communal lunches and tea parties were held on the streets of Seaton. In Britain's time-honoured way of signalling victory since the Armada, massive bonfires were lit on prominent sites and a tremendous feeling of relief spread over Seaton and the whole of East Devon.

The dropping of the atomic bombs during August 1945 saw the end of war with Japan. Once again, a two-day national holiday was declared and street parties were held throughout the town. The bells of St Gregory's rang out and the general rejoicing ended on the second night, when the entire town gathered on the seafront. During that evening, a Japanese prisoner of war, who had returned early to his hometown of Seaton—a young soldier who was a member of the Rogers family—was chair-lifted and carried shoulder-high through the cheering crowd. Once again, the chairman of the council, Frank Norcombe, proved his worth by leading the town, not only in the joyous celebrations that took place, but also in the Christian act of thanksgiving.

The Final Victory

This is the village where I work at

SOUVENIR PROGRAMME

BEER VICTORY CELEBRATIONS

V

SATURDAY, JUNE 8TH, 1946

Right: Programme for Beer Victory Celebrations, 1946.

Below: Major Peter G. V. Bellers saw action in Burma, and this Welcome Home was sent to all who had served, from the Seaton Urban District Council.

Your friends and neighbours in your Home Town
welcome you home
and thank you for the part you played
in helping
to save Our Country from its great peril

P. G. V. BELLERS.

SEATON, DEVON
1946

VE Day, Tuesday 8 May 1945. This was the day for which they had all waited. We had won the war after nearly six weary years of fighting. Here we see the street party held in Highwell Road, Seaton, to celebrate the great victory. Standing on the left is the Seaton vicar, Revd H. R. Cooke, MC, who would have paid a visit to the many street parties held on that day.

In the immediate post-war period, the Seaton branch of the British Legion played an important role in the town. In partnership with the football club, they restarted the Seaton Carnival. Legion members also organised the Seaton Regatta and the Seaton Autumn Show. Bill Hatchley, the vice-chairman of the branch, was the main mover and his early death in 1951 robbed the town of a very able organiser.

Conclusion

May and June 2005, sixty years since the end of the Second World War, has brought back so many vivid memories of what life was like in this East Devon town at that time. Of course, Seaton's role in the war will not feature prominently, if at all, in major historical accounts, and the town's experiences of that era are not in any case dissimilar to those of many other small south coast communities that faced the peril of air raids and invasion. Other towns welcomed evacuees, saw the arrival of allied troops from overseas, witnessed the establishment of internment camps and experienced moments of heroism, stoicism and fortitude. But the wartime story of each town is different and unique. Memories of 1939–45 are important to the shared identity and heritage of a particular community. They need to be recorded before they are lost. In a small way, therefore, I hope that these words have made their contribution to the recollection of a time that has shaped this town and its people and in whose honour it is offered.

Museum Curator Ted Gosling and then Seaton Town Mayor Bob Palacio welcomed former US Army Colonel John Rudman to Seaton in August 2010. John Rudman was interested to see where his father, Robert G. Rudman, who served with the 2nd Battalion 8th Infantry Division of the US Army, had lived and trained in the run up to the D-Day invasion.

Ted took John Rudman around Seaton and pointed out the various places where the Americans were billeted, and said that he regretted that the town did not have a permanent memorial to the many GIs who were stationed in Seaton during the Second World War.

As a result of this visit, Col. Rudman arranged for the Museum to receive the national flag of the United States, the Stars and Stripes, which had flown over the White House in honour of the people of Seaton. They also sent a Congressional Record, and both items are on permanent display in the Museum. The pictures show the flag in its amazing display case, and the framed Record.

Seaton and East Devon in the Second World War

The Final Victory

I WISH TO MARK, BY THIS PERSONAL MESSAGE, my appreciation of the service you have rendered to your Country in 1939.

In the early days of the War you opened your door to strangers who were in need of shelter, & offered to share your home with them.

I know that to this unselfish task you have sacrificed much of your own comfort, & that it could not have been achieved without the loyal co-operation of all in your household.

By your sympathy you have earned the gratitude of those to whom you have shown hospitality, & by your readiness to serve you have helped the State in a work of great value.

Elizabeth R

Mrs. Webster.

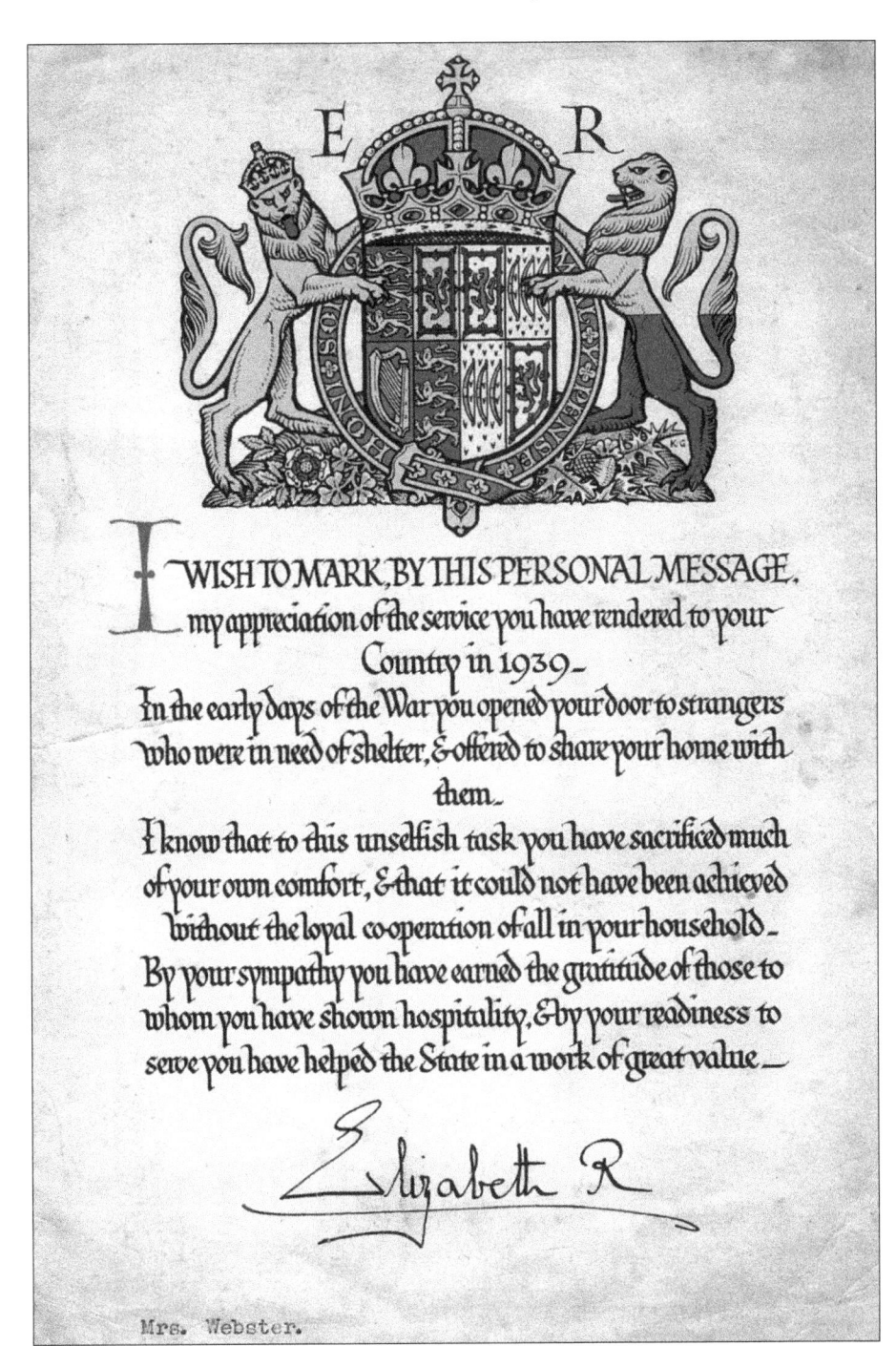

Certificate of appreciation presented to Mrs Webster.

Two local boys, Sgt. Bill Baker and Sgt. Eric Munday, 1st Battalion Grenadier Guards, shortly after the war having served in Palestine and Libya.

Acknowledgements

I am grateful to the many people who have contributed material for this book. Particular thanks to Daphne Harman Young for allowing me to use information from her archives, and to many others who answered my questions about the Second World War. Many books were consulted, too many to mention, but the responsibility for any errors is mine.

Special thanks must go to Geoff and Lyn Marshall, who gave invaluable help in producing this book. I could not have achieved it without them.

I would like to mention the former US Army Colonel John Rudman, whose visit to Seaton was the inspiration for the book.

Thanks to Sarah Parker of Fonthill Media for her help and advice, and I am grateful to my wife Carol for her encouragement and assistance.

My thanks must go to Seaton Town Council for the grant they awarded me for producing this book, and to Cllr Gaynor Sedgwick for the excellent introduction.

We can indeed be thankful that in its darkest hour democracy found two great champions in Churchill and Franklin D. Roosevelt, men of priceless experience and conviction, whose words inspired a generation to stand up against the horrors of dictatorship. The quiet courage of the Second World War generation shone through and showed why this country then deserved to be known as Great Britain.

Ted Gosling
2014